BE FREE

BE FREE

Angela deJong

MOUNTAINS, MISHAPS
AND MIRACLES IN AFRICA

RMB
rmbooks.com

For information on purchasing bulk quantities of this book, or to obtain media excerpts or invite the author to speak at an event, please visit rmbooks.com and select the "Contact" tab.

RMB | Rocky Mountain Books Ltd.
rmbooks.com
@rmbooks
facebook.com/rmbooks

Cataloguing data available from Library and Archives Canada
ISBN 9781771605175 (softcover)
ISBN 9781771605182 (electronic)

Design by Lara Minja, Lime Design

Printed and bound in Canada

We would like to also take this opportunity to acknowledge the traditional territories upon which we live and work. In Calgary, Alberta, we acknowledge the Niitsítapi (Blackfoot) and the people of the Treaty 7 region in Southern Alberta, which includes the Siksika, the Piikuni, the Kainai, the Tsuut'ina, and the Stoney Nakoda First Nations, including Chiniki, Bearpaw, and Wesley First Nations. The City of Calgary is also home to Métis Nation of Alberta, Region III. In Victoria, British Columbia, we acknowledge the traditional territories of the Lkwungen (Esquimalt and Songhees), Malahat, Pacheedaht, Scia'new, T'Sou-ke, and W̱SÁNEC (Pauquachin, Tsartlip, Tsawout, Tseycum) peoples.

We acknowledge the financial support of the Government of Canada through the Canada Book Fund and the Canada Council for the Arts, and of the province of British Columbia through the British Columbia Arts Council and the Book Publishing Tax Credit.

For my incredibly supportive mom and dad.
Thank you for having an unwavering trust in my ability.

I'm sorry for all the sleepless nights.

Contents

Preface

FOR YEARS my friends and family asked me to compile my stories and write this book. With small snapshots of my experiences through email while abroad, I shared tidbits of funny trials and tribulations I had along the way, sparing them the scary details and the moments I knew would forever change me. These are not things you want to dish out online when you're thousands of kilometres away from home, travelling alone.

I had reservations about following through with this book. Part of the beauty of travelling by yourself is having special memories and feelings that are fully appreciated from your own perspective with no input from anyone else to slightly shift your initial impression of the event. I also understand that no matter how you tell a story, it will never resonate like you want it to. Then there is the added nervousness in having others ask innocent questions, or make judgments that could possibly taint your impression. When your memories are so intimate and meaningful, it almost feels disloyal to your soul to say them out loud.

So for a full decade I kept most stories to myself, never anticipating sharing them and being absolutely okay with it. These travel experiences are personal and I don't go for any other reason than to satisfy a draw so intense I feel like I have to. Even before I had ever visited another country, I contemplated why I am so compelled to embark on these journeys. *Am I running away from something? Am I not truly happy? I feel happy, but maybe I'm not? Is there something I'm searching for?* With every adventure it became very clear I was actually running toward the discovery and understanding of who I am as an individual. I believe we learn a lot about our character, what we are capable of and what we value most when we are scared, pressured and solely dependent on our own intuition. This is what travelling alone will offer. It provides the opportunity to grow as an individual physically, mentally and spiritually. It's terrifying, disappointing at times, liberating and addictive!

So, with all that, why am I telling these stories now? Something unexpected happened to me in 2018 that changed my mind. As the saying goes: "never say never."

This book is a compilation of short stories highlighting some of my scariest, most embarrassing and proudest moments. I made some poor choices, took cringe-worthy chances, put trust in people often too soon and suffered a great deal at times when I didn't need to. Every bit of it was worth it. In return, I gained the gifts of resiliency, perspective and gratitude that have enriched my life and made me happier than I ever thought possible.

JORDAN, 2018

◎ **I WAS EN ROUTE TO JORDAN** for another solo hiking trip. It wasn't until then that a conversation with a lovely woman on the airplane challenged my perspective on sharing my adventures. She selflessly told a personal story about her son who had a love for adventure similar to mine, and tragically went missing in the Rocky Mountains. For years they searched, but he was never found. Her story was heart-wrenching, but she told it with such grace. The intention she had in sharing her experience was not to leave me feeling distressed or discouraged from living my dreams but rather to give me some insight into what it's like for loved ones at home to not know or understand what you've been through. "I will never have my son back," she stated, holding back tears, "but I'm so grateful he lived the life he wanted while he was here." I tried to hold myself together while she continued on. "My only regret is that I didn't know more about his adventures. He shared little comments here and there over the years, but never more than that. I wish we had documentation of all his adventurous memories to remind us of what ignited him with passion and to have a better understanding of who he was and why he insisted on testing the limits. We never discouraged him, and I'm glad we didn't, but I never appreciated why he didn't want to go to Mexico and lie on a beach like everyone else. It took me some time, but I have peace knowing he passed doing what he loved most."

We sat quietly for a moment. I needed some time to process what she had shared. I also didn't want to be inconsiderate and ask too many questions, possibly stirring up more sadness. After a few minutes of reflection, the lovely lady broke the awkward silence. "It is not my intention to impose, but you may want to consider writing your adventures down, if you haven't already. I am certain they would inspire people. It would let them into a world that they most likely would never see. I know it would be one of the greatest gifts you could give your parents." It never came up in conversation that I had written books in the past or had decided long ago that I would keep my stories to myself. It felt as though she was looking into the future and could see something I couldn't. Her story and the way she told it resonated very strongly. "I promise I will consider it," I said back, meaning it.

When we said our goodbyes in the airport she gave me a big squeeze and whispered in my ear, "Watch for eagles. My son loved them and considered them good luck. And be safe, my friend. Listen to your head whispers, your gut feeling is always right." Her words had a sincerity to them that made it feel like she was saying goodbye to her son for the last time.

I never caught the lovely lady's name, but I will always remember her. I thought about her experiences and insights a lot during my travels across Jordan. I wondered if her son had ever visited there, or planned to. I kept my eyes open for eagles every day and I appreciated every moment I could.

Each morning in Jordan I had the same routine. It was warm enough at night to sleep without a tent, so all I had to do was slip out of my sleeping bag and walk to a private spot far enough away from camp, careful to not wake my sleeping hiking guide. One particular morning, I had my legs stretched out over a large rock surface while I listened to power ballads and transferred my thoughts and experiences to paper. I set my journal down and looked across the incredible vista before me. We were surrounded with smooth white rock faces highlighted with dancing yellow light cascading across them. Tufts of green shrub sporadically grew between the mountain cracks, making the area seem just a little less harsh and a little more inviting. It was a different kind of beautiful in this region of the world. It was desolate but still stunning. I lost track of time as I scanned for hidden images within the lines and shadows of the mountain. In my almost meditative state it took me a moment to realize that my name was being called over the music. I turned behind me to discover my guide awake and enticing me to come back for breakfast by waving the eggs around. He was smiling from ear to ear and looked excited to start the day. *He's the best – never in a bad mood, that one. And he knows eggs are the way to my heart.* When I turned to pick up my notes next to me, I was stunned by what I saw. An eagle was sitting on top of them looking out at the same beautiful landscape I was scanning a moment ago. He looked directly at me for just a second and then casually flew off. It was the only eagle I spotted in four weeks. *Did that just happen? No. That's crazy! Was that a good sign or a bad sign?*

◎ **I DON'T BELIEVE THINGS HAPPEN BY ACCIDENT** – there is always a reason or a lesson. I could have sat next to anyone on the airplane and consequently had a different experience in Jordan, and then gone home to never tell my tales. This book is in large part due to the openness of a kind stranger. It's fitting because, as you'll see, that is a common theme within almost every story. It's never the hiking or the adventure that ends up making the trip memorable, although that is what I'd lead you to believe if we spoke about it; it's just easier that way. In actuality, it's the people and the deep connections you form under extraordinary circumstances that leave the lasting impression. I'm so grateful for every single individual I have met along the way – even the ones that scared me. I have learned a lot through listening, observing, trusting and being vulnerable.

Speaking of being vulnerable...let's go! Or as they say in Jordan, *yalla*!

KENYA

Approximately 4:30 a.m.

WELL, SHIT, I THOUGHT TO MYSELF. The tinfoil blanket flapped aggressively above our heads as my guide Samuel and I huddled under it in an effort to protect us from the ruthless snowstorm. I was literally between a rock (a large one) and a hard place (a mountainside with a serious weather system leaving us with zero visibility). Samuel and I were face to face, eye to eye, breathing visible frosty air on one another's faces, attempting to remain calm and warm at an elevation around 4800 m.

When we left camp at around 3:00 a.m. the sky was impeccably clear and speckled with millions of flickering stars. The moon appeared to be so close and its brightness helped create a daunting silhouette of the towering mountain ahead of us. At departure there were no signs of rain or snow to come. But within only an hour clouds flooded the sky and quickly produced precipitation that transitioned into snow. It churned around us and began to accumulate quickly. In a very short period of time, the visibility had degraded to a level where I could no longer see Samuel in front of me – at all. I had to step into each individual footprint he made in the ankle-deep powder to stay the course. It would have been less nerve-racking had I been ignorant of the

fact that there was a serious cliff to our left. I had an approxima-
tion of how close we were in relationship to it, so navigating over
every slippery jagged rock required extra focus and deliberate
foot placement as a precaution. We found ourselves in a sticky
situation where it was eventually too unsafe to continue to the
summit, but it was also very risky to head back to camp. Samuel
admitted he did not know if we were still on course, so he recommended we wait for a break in the weather to safely continue
in either direction.

Every year for the past decade I'd saved my vacation time and
money to fly back to my favourite place on the planet: Africa. I'd
had multiple things go wrong, endless problems and worries, but
I always had a strong feeling it would all work out – and it did.
For the first time I wasn't sure I was getting out of this one. *So
this is how it's going to end?* I thought to myself. *Everyone warned
me that I only had so many chances, so many lives before something
terrible would happen. Is this it?* I think some of my negativity
stemmed from the altitude but mostly from the unwavering
focus that Samuel had on me. He never said it, but he didn't need
to because his eyes had "I'm so sorry" flooding them. My guide
was losing confidence. This was a bad situation.

We slid behind a large boulder to protect ourselves from the
wind. The solid rock gave me an odd sense of security, that I was
leaning away from the cliff that was hiding just a few mysterious feet away. I pulled out my tinfoil blanket and then Samuel
and I sat on our backpacks in every effort to save our body heat.
The slope we were perched on was unnerving and a constant
reminder of just how close we were to the edge. I dug the heels
of my boots into the snow and scree beneath them to feel a little
more secure.

With below-freezing temperatures, a vicious howling wind and
a lack of movement, Samuel and I had to rely on each other to
stay warm. Our heads were pressed up against one another as we

wrapped our arms around each other to contain as much body heat between us as possible. Initially, we sat in silence. I think we both needed several minutes to process the severity of the situation and manage our emotions. Then, out of nowhere, Samuel spoke. "Anyela,[1] tell me about your times in Africa. Please." To this day I don't know the reasoning behind his request, but I assumed it was to provide the distraction we both needed. I had no desire to talk, let alone tell stories, but I knew it was important that I did. "Where do you want me to begin?" I asked, with a little hesitation in my voice. "From the start. What was your first time to Africa like?" he said, knowing we had some time.

---

1   Wherever I travelled in Africa, this is how my named sounded when spoken.

TANZANIA

"IS HE OKAY?" I asked with serious concern about my hiking guide Moses.

"His head is very bad. He cannot go on," Roger, the young cook, explained.

"He is not doing enough sport," the park ranger, Godfrey, interjected insensitively.

"Do you feel sick, Moses?" I asked, in worry with regard to the altitude. Moses nodded his head and blinked slowly.

"He must do more exercise. Huh. He is so lazy," the park ranger continued with judgment and coldness in his heart.

"I think it is the altitude," Roger corrected him.

"Then I believe he must go down," the ranger dictated as he sneered at Moses.

I was familiar with the risks of hiking above 2500 m, but never imagined I'd see them first-hand, let alone days into my trip. Shortness of breath, headaches, dizziness, fatigue, loss of appetite and difficulty sleeping: all were early symptoms of something that could become more serious. I knew that continuing to climb in elevation while ignoring the initial warning symptoms could lead to serious health concerns such as fluid around the lungs or even the brain. It was imperative that Moses descend the mountain and receive medical attention. My first trip to Africa was already providing challenges I didn't expect, and lessons I never imagined.

◎ **MY INITIAL INTENTION** upon arrival in Tanzania was to hire residents in the nearby city of Arusha to guide me up Kilimanjaro. It was an attempt to support local business rather than large foreign companies, but "Kili" is regulated by the government and requires licensed staff and rangers to hike it. Since I arrived without a tour group (or game plan), I had to catch a ride to the Kilimanjaro National Park gate to arrange a hiking crew on-site. I had no idea what I was getting myself into until I stepped out of the taxi and approached a lineup of nearly two-dozen men hoping to be selected for a trekking gig.

I didn't want to offend anyone, but I had no clue what criteria made someone "look" to be a suitable guide, so I started at one end of the line and slowly made my way down, shaking every gentleman's hand trying to get an impression. In the end, I based my uncomfortable selection on two superficial measures:

1. **SMILE:** Was it a forced, fake smile, or one that came from their eyes and felt genuine?
2. **HANDSHAKE:** Was it firm with confidence, or too firm, making it feel arrogant or macho?

I awkwardly pointed to the sturdy-looking gentleman in the blue knit sweater who was the only one that made eye contact with me. He had a warm smile and a quiet confidence about him that I liked. "Would you like to hike Kilimanjaro with me?" I asked sheepishly. The formality made it feel like a rose ceremony on the hit television show *The Bachelorette*, but with less makeup and more DEET. Moses smiled and giggled a little as he responded with his yes. My insecurities got the better of me, making me question whether he was laughing in delight or laughing at me for doing something silly I was not aware of. It was an adjustment to be the minority and wanting to fit in, but not being fully capable of communicating due to the language barrier.

It was a relief when I observed Moses selecting a cook and a porter for our team, saving me the pressure. He didn't walk the line, but he pointed out his selections like I did, which made me feel a little more confident I hadn't embarrassed myself with my process. Based on their friendly exchange, I suspected they might have been friends or colleagues he worked well with in the past. The final addition to our crew was Godfrey, a park ranger the national park headquarters selected. It was explained to me that his role was to protect us from potential animals in the area. He was the smallest ranger of the group, standing at about five feet two inches tall, but he had a look of ferocity on his face that made him seem bigger and more terrifying. I intentionally observed the other rangers to see if perhaps they were all trained to have this scary persona. The laughing and friendly hand slapping were clear indicators that the hostility was not a ranger characteristic – it was a Godfrey characteristic. *Egad! I hope he loosens up a bit. He's a little bit scary.*

When the crew was finalized, I introduced myself to everyone in an effort to make things as comfortable as possible. The young cook Roger vigorously shook my hand with excitement. He explained in broken English that it would be his first trek up Kilimanjaro too. The porter Henry looked to be about 50 and was very shy. He wouldn't look up at me as he shook my hand, but he seemed to be a kind gentleman. The park ranger squeezed my hand so hard I thought he was intentionally trying to hurt me. He didn't say anything and just stared, making it feel like an unnecessary intimidation technique. I couldn't tell if he was threatened by me, or if he just hated me. Either way, we were not off to a good start. He certainly would not be getting my first impression rose!

I was told at the park gates that for every hiker it was mandatory to have a minimum of four people (one guide, one ranger, one cook and one porter) escort you up the mountain, for safety purposes. I wasn't sure if the information was true or if it was simply a way to employ four people. Either way, I was completely okay with it as long as they honoured my one request to carry my own backpack. This is an essential factor for my hiking enjoyment: to test my body and fitness level with elevation gain paired with the extra satisfaction of transporting my own equipment. I know it might sound weird, but it's my thing. Right away the guys grabbed my bag and put it on the scale to confirm it was less than the 33 pounds permitted. To my delight, it made the cut by half a pound. But then it got me thinking, *Damn it! I could have packed that jar of peanut butter I wanted after all.*

It may have been the language barrier, or perhaps the guys simply could not comprehend why, but my bag became a small argument. I tried to explain myself, but I couldn't help but think they thought I didn't trust them with my belongings. "I trust you. I just like to exercise and work hard," I explained as simply (although ineffectively) as I could. The park ranger stomped up to me and yelled when he spoke, "You cannot carry the bag. It is very difficult and you will not make it." I was completely offended, yet very aware that he knew a lot more about what we were about to embark on than I did, so doubt crept in. I left the conversation for a moment to think about how important this factor was for me. *Is this worth an argument? You just met these guys. Do you really want to make a big deal of this? What if you end up not being able to do it and you look like an idiot?* I had only been in Africa for about 48 hours and I was already questioning myself.

In the end I reminded myself of why I was here and what would make me happiest. It was simple: to take the hardest route up possible, and carry my own bag. I get pleasure out of being uncomfortable; I believe it's how we grow as individuals. The more I thought about it, the more it became a non-negotiable for me. I realized I was risking looking like a complete idiot if I ended up having to give my bag up to be successful, but the chance was worth it.

The guys were frantically weighing, packing and passing gear around. I felt awkward and a little unwelcome in the group, but I needed to say something before they divided up my things between them. "Let me try to carry the bag. If I can't, I will give it up," I said as assertively as I could. Nobody heard me. *Okay, more assertive Ang! It's okay to ask for what you want! You've made a lot of sacrifice to be here. Try to do it your way.* I had the pep talk in my head and tried again. "Guys!" I yelled out to get their attention. *Crap, everyone is staring at me.* "I...I." *Say something you nitwit!* "I am carrying my bag," I said sternly. *Well done, Ang.* I complimented myself in my head for doing something uncomfortable.

"No," was the response I got from the park ranger. I don't know how I did it, but the words just came out: "Then I won't go." I walked away from the situation to keep myself composed and to avoid any further argument. The people-pleaser in me was going squirrelly, but this was a deal-breaker issue for me. I knew I looked like a fool trying to negotiate something that would make my trek more difficult, potentially risking my chances of success, but it was a detail I wasn't willing to budge on. The guys whispered among themselves while I tried not to worry about what they thought of me. It would have been easy to let my mind go to the negative, but I reeled it in as best I could. *Talk about it all you want guys. I know I can carry my own bag.*

Godfrey refused to talk to me, and sent Moses instead. "I am sorry to cause any conflict. I just want to enjoy the hike. For me, this means having the satisfaction of carrying my own bag." With the language barrier in mind, I tried to explain myself as best I could. "I know I look silly. But please let me try. It is important," I added when he didn't respond right away. "You like sport?" he asked. "Yes, very much," I confirmed, hoping this meant he was starting to understand. "Okay. It will be very hard. But you can try." He gave in, but I could tell he wasn't convinced. I didn't like the feeling of having to prove myself, but it was understandable considering they didn't know me at all. To them I was just another tourist they wanted to help successfully summit. In a way, I was potentially making their job more stressful, maybe even more dangerous. All I was asking for was the chance to try. "Thank you, Moses. This means a lot," I responded back. "Be free," he said with a smile.

If you ever visit Africa, you are likely to hear these words. They are often used to make someone feel welcome or comfortable. Be free: relax, you are welcome here, do as you like, be yourself, enjoy.

I walked past Godfrey, looking right at him while he immaturely pretended not to see me. I picked up my bag and slung it on my back, appreciating how right it felt. I caught the ranger looking at me with disgust as I clipped the belt on. He shook his head and began ordering the other guys around for what looked like no apparent reason other than to satisfy his chipped ego.

We hadn't even left the Umbwe trail entry gate before I found myself in another disagreement. "Is that table and chair for me?" I asked the guide, flabbergasted, knowing the answer. It was a solid wood table large enough to accommodate six people and a green plastic chair. "Yes, so you can eat," he replied back, surprised by the question. "I don't need a table and chair all to myself. Where will you all eat? There's only one chair," I pointed out and questioned the logic behind this. "The ground," he said, like it was obvious. "I can sit on the ground too," I said happily. He paused for a moment and then hesitated with his answer. "What is it?" I asked, realizing there was something I was missing. "It is his job," he pointed as he spoke. It became apparent that, if I didn't use the table and chair, Henry would be out of a job. I was trying to do the right thing, but in actuality I didn't understand the system and the impact on everyone involved. I thought quickly on my feet. "Okay, Henry can come with us, but he doesn't need to carry the table and chair," I insisted. Moses was speechless again. "You will pay him to take nothing?" he said with a laugh. "Yes. I came to Africa to meet locals and learn about Africa. How can I do that sitting alone at a table for six?" I explained. Moses smiled wide, "Really? Okay, you will learn about Africa. We will teach you. You are welcome." He said it in disbelief, but happily.

The look on Henry's face when it was explained to him that he would be hiking with us but not expected to carry anything was priceless. Godfrey piped in quickly to say, "Very soon you will carry her bag. She will see. It is very difficult. It is too hard." Then he smiled at me in a way that was condescending and yet motivating. *My stubbornness might just kill me on this mountain. I will do everything in my power to prove this awful dude wrong. On the other hand, he has unknowingly provided me a little comfort, suggesting I have an out with my bag if I need one. But I won't. I don't think. I hope.*

The day's walk began on slippery red clay, scattered with leaves and twigs. The canopy of trees was thick, rich and green, and we had the entire side of the mountain to ourselves. The hike was a slow steady incline for the first hour, which was a huge help in easing my body and mind into the experience. Doubt surged in and out of my mind as to whether I was being foolish carrying my own bag. Periodically, Godfrey would make a discouraging comment or two to get at me. *"Tsst,* that bag...it's too heavy. Too big." I used his snide remarks to fuel the fire inside me, to push even harder. *I think I'm doing just fine so far, thank you very much. My legs are feeling strong and my backpack feels great!*

The final two and half hours of the day were spent climbing a natural staircase made from roots and rocks. It was as if Mother Nature carved stairs out of the clay and the tree roots were left to reinforce them, preventing erosion. My legs felt strong and my heart pounded in my chest like it did at home on the stair-climber in the gym. I found myself leaping from one stair to the next with absolute joy. I was in the company of one bad apple, but three lovely gentlemen compensated for him. "You cannot do it. You will be tired. Slow down," Godfrey yelled up at me as I bounded up and around the corner, leaving him in my dust. It was unlike me to not follow the rules, but he had lost my respect within ten minutes of us meeting, and I didn't want to be around his energy any longer than I had to.

I wasn't the only one he picked on. Moses became a target periodically as well. "Why are you so slow? Are you a guide?" he would comment meanly. Moses was very slow and intentional with his steps, but I assumed it was his way of managing the altitude or perhaps he had a nagging injury. He never defended himself; he just maintained his consistent pace with class and tried to ignore Godfrey like I did.

When we arrived in our first camp, Moses, Roger and Henry were noticeably behind Godfrey and me. Nearly 45 minutes later they made their arrival. "I am the ranger and the guide today. You are too slow to be the guide," Godfrey unkindly said to Moses. It wasn't obvious that Moses was upset about the comments or the circumstances. He had little expression on his face, which made me think he was simply too tired to have one. I thought perhaps a good night's sleep would rejuvenate him for day two.

The next morning Moses and I departed camp, just the two of us, a little earlier than the rest of the crew. He made a comment before we left that it would be a "little break." I knew he was referring to Godfrey. His arrogance and nasty comments were clearly unpleasant for everyone.

That morning the two of us steadily climbed for four hours. I loved it! Some of the areas were really steep, requiring us to use our hands and feet to ascend, while others were simply slow and steady natural rock stairs. Moses struggled with his breathing, blaming it on the off-season hiatus he'd had.

The frequent rest periods seemed to help Moses, which was wonderful, but it also gave the other guys plenty of time to catch us. This stressed me out because I felt the need to prove Godfrey wrong. "See. You are tired and need too many rests. I know these things. You cannot carry that bag. You are a woman," Godfrey barked at me as he walked up the trail to join us. *So that's why you don't think I can do it! Well crap, now I really have to prove you're wrong!* "Anyela is very strong. It is me she is waiting for," Moses defended me unselfishly. I didn't say anything, but my respect for him grew even more. Moses had climbed Mount Kilimanjaro hundreds of times and when he spoke about it a glow of pride radiated. "When you beat Kilimanjaro, this feeling is very, very good. You will see."

Today, unfortunately, he appeared to be struggling, and Kilimanjaro was winning. Our pace was painfully slow, and he could see I was anxious to go faster but didn't want to leave him and disobey the hiking rule: keep near your guide at all times. As a compromise, he suggested I run up ahead for 30 minutes and then wait to meet as a group, for safety purposes. I was thrilled with the suggestion, but in hindsight I was ignorant of the idea that perhaps his struggles were due to altitude, not deconditioning like he was thinking. It never occurred to me that my veteran hiking guide might be the one to get sick, especially so early on.

After several bursts of hiking then waiting, Moses finally suggested I finish the day's trip with Godfrey where we could wait and relax in the camp. He explained that he would catch up to us in his own time, along with the cook and the porter. It must have killed him to make that decision, especially after all the horrible accusations Godfrey had made about him being an unfit guide. Like the true gentleman he was, he put all that aside for my experience to be great. Part of me wanted to go for it; another part didn't want to be alone with Godfrey. Moses pulled me aside and gave me a little encouragement. "If you go at your pace, he will not talk. He is very tired. I can see this with my eyes." Moses was correct! Godfrey didn't say a word the entire time. He pushed to keep up, and he did, but it was an effort for him. I wanted so badly to make a comment on how he had Henry carry his bag for him, but I thought better of that idea very quickly. I knew there would be no winning with Godfrey. When we made it into camp, he lay down on the ground and didn't move for the entire duration of my tent set up, snack and one chapter of my book. I secretly took a photo of him lying in a heap to remind me to trust my ability and never let anyone cause me to question it again.

It was over an hour and a half before Moses and the two other fellas met us. Moses looked defeated and absolutely exhausted. His steps were more like shuffles and his shoulders were slumped so far over you couldn't even see his face. Immediately, I knew this was more than a lack of fitness; he was obviously sick. It was a wake-up call to see that experience was not a guarantee for success. I learned that some days you can be virtually unaffected and others the altitude can cripple you.

Moses stumbled over toward us and sat on the ground next to me. His breathing was shallow and he was having a hard time sitting up. Rupert and Henry went straight into organization mode and began to prepare hot water for tea. Godfrey looked unimpressed and did nothing but clean under his fingernails with his pocketknife. I immediately went to my bag in search of my altitude sickness medication. I knew that it was intended for prophylactic measures, but I thought there was no harm in him taking it now, just in case it helped even a tiny bit. Moses accepted it gratefully, gently sipped more water, and then hung his head down in pain. I'd never been in this position before, let alone in a foreign country with three gentlemen and one jerk I'd just met.

Oops, did that come out? I didn't want to offend anyone, be disrespectful in any way or step on anyone's toes, but I also didn't want Moses to keep hiking in an effort to keep his guiding payment. I graciously asked Rupert, Godfrey and Henry to give me a moment with Moses alone. The three of them left – two with no issues, and one clearly pissed off. I sat next to Moses and did my best to explain my concern without sounding like I was some new Kilimanjaro altitude expert that knew better than he did. I was sad that my decision would likely impact my attempt at the summit in the morning, but I didn't trust that he would put himself before me, so I knew I had to say it. "Moses, your health is more important than this hike," I said. He looked up at me and shook his head in disagreement. "Please. Let me say something," I asserted. "I know you want me to succeed, but I can't keep hiking knowing it might cause you more harm," I explained. "It is my job, Anyela. I must work for my family," he pleaded. Once again I was trying my best to do what I thought was right, but somehow I was making a mess of it. I thought quickly on my feet for a solution. "No matter what, I'm paying you for five days guiding as we agreed. But promise me we will all go down tonight." He nodded his head with sincere appreciation in his eyes.

We sat for a few minutes quietly, reflecting. I was relieved and saddened all at the same time, but I knew it was the right decision. I tried to lighten the mood with a dumb random comment: "You know, I think my feet are really going to stink when I take off my boots." Moses laughed out loud with surprise then cleverly added, "You are very strong, Anyela. Maybe your feet are too." "Do you think I should wave them around Godfrey? They might knock him out!" I asked with a cheeky grin. "I think this is a very good idea!" Moses commented. "Do it quickly. I very much hope he stops talking." We laughed for a moment, and then sat quietly again. It was heartbreaking to know how much he was suffering.

Hesitantly, Moses broke the silence. "Maybe you could still summit. Would it be okay if Godfrey or Rupert guided you tomorrow?" It was Rupert's first time on Mount Kilimanjaro and Godfrey was a nightmare to be around, so my options were less than ideal, but at least I might have a shot.

Without hesitation, Rupert accepted the opportunity happily. Godfrey agreed, but not without celebrating his new self-made title as "first guide and best ranger."

"I will radio for help. Someone will come to get me," Moses announced almost immediately after knowing we had a plan, making it even more apparent just how much pain he was in.

It was around 11 p.m. when the rescue crew jogged into our camp to assist Moses with his descent. Godfrey tried to boss everyone around, but he was ignored. Apparently, we weren't the only ones that thought he was quite rude. One of the rangers slung Moses over his shoulders and proceeded to jog down the mountain. It would have been impressive at any time, but with Moses in particular it was awe-inspiring. The gentleman doing the transporting had an impressive-sized fella on him! It was decided that Henry would go down with the crew in case additional assistance was required. I believe now this is a big part of why the Tanzanian government insists on having at least four people to every one tourist.

The men were in and out in an astoundingly quick time. Altitude sickness is very serious and moving to lower elevation provides the best chance for recovery. Before they left, they assured us Moses would be okay and that we'd made the right decision to have him escorted down. Godfrey interjected and insisted it was all his idea. It was his idea, nobody was disputing that, but he insisted on making sure everyone knew, just in case. Our group of five was quickly down to two plus one asshole. If there were to be a "Women Tell All" episode of *The Bachelorette*, that statement would sure fire up Bachelor Nation!

I heard a tentative tapping on my tent early the next morning. I opened up the door to see smiling Rupert holding a cup of tea and a plate of *chapatti* (a flatbread). I felt absolutely spoiled to have breakfast made for me. Moses and I had left so early the previous day we missed breakfast. I'd never hiked or camped with a guide or cook before, so everything was new and surprising. I crawled out of my quarters and sat contently on a folded tarp Rupert meticulously laid out on a large rock. I was in awe of the unobstructed view of Mount Kilimanjaro's peak directly in front of me. The glacier was bright white, causing me to put my sunglasses on to appreciate it. I shrunk up as I watched Godfrey approach me. He stood awkwardly close, making it feel like he was trying to intimidate me. If that was his plan, it was working, but I tried desperately not to let it show. "Want some chapatti?" I offered politely, thinking it might make him go away. He responded by pulling the tinfoil out of my hands and taking it all, including the one I had started to nibble on. Rupert saw the entire interaction, but he was too scared to say anything. Moses had the experience and enough presence to keep Godfrey in line a little. We didn't know it at the time, but now it was obvious just how much worse he could be.

◎ **IT WAS DAY THREE** on the Umbwe trail and our condensed team finally met up with other trekkers. It was here where all of the routes eventually collided and melded into one approach to tackle the famous Barranco Wall. It was a fairly direct route up, but not very challenging cardiovascular-wise compared to the day prior. The view from the top was spectacular! In the distance was Mount Meru, Africa's second-highest peak.

The remainder of the day was a slow slog as we walked politely behind some of the other hikers. Rupert knew the pace was not my first choice so he joked with me, "*Pole, pole* [slowly, slowly in Swahili]...there is no disco at the camp, Simba [lion]." I smiled and joked back, "Rupert, we could make one happen. I've got great tunes!" He shook his hips back and forth like he was dancing and waved his hands in the air. Then he went back to whistling his cheerful song that he periodically treated me with. Godfrey trailed behind us quietly most of the day, making it feel that much more pleasant.

When we arrived at camp, Rupert and I set up our tents and waited for Godfrey to arrive. We had a picnic pasta dinner under the stars and went to bed early in anticipation of our 12:00 a.m. summit departure. I pulled Rupert aside and told him that I would really like to hike at our pace, so leaving first would be optimal, not to be held up by anyone. He nodded his head, but I wasn't sure he fully understood what I was asking. Our communication was stunted at times due to my Swahili speaking inadequacy and his limited English.

I froze that night and didn't sleep a wink. My equipment was of poor quality and I believe the altitude was also a factor. I had barely eaten any of my pasta earlier and I was starting to have concerns I would not have the energy to summit. My mind was taking a negative turn and I was questioning my ability to perform. I'd never been at this altitude before (4672 m) and I had no idea how my body would respond going even higher. I felt vulnerable and anxious about failing at something that I normally would feel confident about. I wasn't thinking like my usual self. Perhaps it was the unknown, perhaps it was the elements that I could not control and perhaps it was the altitude playing tricks on my brain or a combination of all three. Regardless, I was going to make the attempt, but that was the only certainty I had. In an effort to stay calm, I kept reminding myself, *it's just one step at a time.*

I was lying in my tent with every item of clothing I had with me on. One pair of regular hiking pants, one pair of fleece pants underneath, one pair of rain pants to block the wind, two long-sleeve shirts, one sweater, one down coat that cost me $17 on sale at Superstore, one raincoat to block the wind, a balaclava, a tuque, two pairs of wool socks, one pair of mitts and a headlamp. Stiff from clothing restriction, I awkwardly sat up like the Michelin Man and packed my backpack with a few snacks and my water bottle. I put my hiking boots on at precisely 12:00 a.m.

so Rupert and I could set off ahead of the other ten tourists that were camping around us. I stepped out of my tent and looked up at the crystal clear sky cluttered with bright stars. There was Orion right above my head! Kilimanjaro gifted me the best starry night I've ever seen to this day.

One by one the other tourists left with their guides to head up toward the peak. Rupert and Godfrey were late. At 12:20 a.m. they came out of their tents while I tried to appreciate the sky instead of being upset about not having the trail to navigate at the pace I desired. *What a diva I am! This is NOT the end of the world. Chill out.* In no time we caught up to the other groups and were walking heel to heel at a particularly slow pace behind everyone, listening to complaints about how steep it was. "It is Kilimanjaro, what did you expect?" one guide said to his clients, making me and Rupert laugh. This was not my idea of a good time, but I tried to focus on my other senses to redirect my thoughts.

The atmosphere was extremely quiet at times, when the wind would die down. I focused on the sounds of rustling rain pants and the *click, click* of hiking poles on the rocks. It was soothing and felt meditative. Then it wasn't. My mind shifted back to our pace and my desire to kick things up a notch. My body felt strong and I was feeling confident again about my ability. Rupert was getting antsy, too, so he took charge and asked to pass the group. Godfrey lost interest in the climb at that point and opted to turn back toward camp. I immediately felt free again. Free to move, free of Godfrey's negative energy. I didn't care about reaching the summit first. The pace wasn't about competition; it was the desire to use my body to its fullest potential and feel it work. The journey up, feeling my calves burn, my heart pound, my feet digging in for traction and my mind so focused – that's what I live for! The grind, the struggle and the discovery of what I'm really made of mentally and physically. To me, the summit was just a destination. The journey was the fun part!

Rupert began to slow down and groan a lot. We had approximately one and a half hours left (but we didn't know that at the time) and I wasn't sure if he was going to make it. Every ten minutes Rupert would lean over and put his hands on his knees to rest in that position for a few minutes. Trekking at high altitudes is not a solo activity; it's a team sport. I learned this earlier from Moses. It was time to take a break and assess whether this was altitude sickness or expected fatigue. I opened up a Twix bar and shared one half with Rupert, paying close attention to his breathing and behaviour like I had with Moses. We sat down and took a few sips of water (our first of the day). Within a few minutes he perked up and started to whistle, like he did earlier in the trek. It was a relief to know he wasn't suffering from the altitude as much as he was suffering from hunger and dehydration.

Once he felt ready to go again, we slowed our pace and pushed on one methodical step at a time, just to be on the safe side. The final stretch toward the summit was surreal. Mount Meru was at our front left, saying hello through pastel pink and orange clouds. To our right was a beautiful volcanic rock valley next to the crater rim. Behind us was the golden sun rising up in preparation to light our way down. And to our front right was Uhuru Peak marking the roof of Africa at 5860 m.

Tears froze to my eyelashes as I walked side by side with Rupert toward the sign. I was so happy it was just the two of us. Upon our arrival, Rupert opened his arms and gave me a huge bear hug and spoke into my ear, "Congratulations, little Simba. You did it." I congratulated him back, since it was his first summit too. We only spent three days together, but we had developed a mutual respect for one another. We took a few photos next to the iconic sign before the two of us froze from the intense wind. It was cold for me and I was used to −35 degrees Celsius, being a Canadian. Rupert was experiencing the same temperatures, but for the first time in his life, and he couldn't quite comprehend what he was feeling. He couldn't get off the summit fast enough!

The descent to camp was a direct route through volcanic scree. We slid through it like we were skiing. The sun was fully up and the sky didn't have a hint of cloud. It was a glorious morning.

When we arrived back to our tents, Godfrey had packed his belongings and nothing else. I took down all three tents while Rupert made more chapatti and tea. Godfrey did absolutely nothing, but at least this time he wasn't talking.

With fuel in our bellies, and adrenaline in our system, the descent went quickly. All three of us ran down the side of Kilimanjaro negotiating scree and small stones. The terrain quickly turned to larger rocks and roots with small vegetation surrounding us. With just two hours left to reach the park gate, Rupert expressed concerns about getting in trouble if anyone found out we had completed the trek in four days, instead of the recommended five. I wasn't sure how valid his worry was, but I was happy to stay one more night on Kilimanjaro to ease his concerns. By this time, Godfrey was still around, but he was no longer talking to us. He appeared to be putting in his time, and doing as little as he possibly could to be around us. Rupert suspected it had something to do with him not summiting with us, and I stopped thinking about him almost completely.

The weather was beautiful that night, so Rupert and I didn't even put up our tents. We laid our sleeping bags out on the forest floor and stared at the stars through the canopy of trees. Listening to the hum of insects, the rustling of monkeys in the foliage and the trickle of water from the passing stream, it was a perfect final night on Kilimanjaro.

Upon our arrival at the park gate, we were met by Moses. It was wonderful to see him healthy and well again. He gave Rupert and me a big hug in congratulations and tried to acknowledge

Godfrey at the same time, but he had walked off to visit with two other rangers standing nearby.

Moses walked me over to the road to show me where I would catch my ride back to Arusha. While we waited, I passed him four envelopes of money, one for each of the guys to provide a little extra thank you for their service. Moses opened the envelope marked with his name on it right away, making me feel very awkward. The only information I had about what was considered a "good" gratuity was what I had read in my travel book. I took that information and doubled it for each of the men, hoping it would please them. Moses was thrilled! I fully understood it wasn't his fault he was unable to complete the hike, so it felt fair to tip him, as I would have under normal circumstances.

Rupert received the largest tip. He not only climbed Kilimanjaro for the first time but he also guided me up safely, cooked lovely meals for all of us and acted as a great neutralizer for Godfrey's negative energy. I was so grateful for him. Henry was not around, but I trusted Moses would pass the envelope along to him. When Godfrey noticed the guys opening their envelopes he coincidently became interested in standing with us. Moses passed him his envelope and he tore it open immediately. He counted the money, making sure everyone could see it all, and appeared to be initially very pleased with the gift. I was relieved I was able to show my appreciation in some way, and they were all happy with the gesture.

The trip would have ended on a very nice note if it hadn't been for Godfrey's ego. He noticed Rupert's envelope in his hand and decided to swipe it from him. He opened it up and counted the money to compare. I was stunned. After going back and forth on my decision all afternoon, I had decided to give Rupert a few dollars more than Godfrey for several reasons: he worked harder, I knew he wasn't paid very well in comparison to a park ranger salary, he was kind and I liked him more. Godfrey's energy shifted back to a dark place, and I could see rage building behind his eyes. He was no longer satisfied with his tip, knowing he received less than Rupert. He took a few bills from the pile and threw the remaining ones back at Rupert's feet. I was appalled by his actions and wanted to grab the money back for Rupert, but I was scared to. Godfrey's actions were not normal and I was worried about what he might do if I pushed back. Clearly just as nervous and disappointed, Moses whispered, "He is no good. Stay away. I am sorry Anyela." He then opened up his envelope and handed Rupert a few bills to replace the ones that were taken.

Rupert and Moses walked me over to a covered shelter to avoid the sun while I waited for the bus. They stayed for a little while and then eventually meandered over to the other park rangers just a few metres away to visit and pass time. I pulled out my journal to make notes about the summit hike and the rewarding sunrise. In the middle of my thoughts I was interrupted by the sound of gravel crackling underneath boots. I looked up to see Godfrey staring down at me with indignation. I stood up right away, feeling the need to protect myself. Before I could run or say a word, Godfrey lurched forward and wrapped his hands around my neck. He squeezed it and pushed me up against the wooden wall. His face was just below mine as he lifted me off the ground. I couldn't breathe. He whispered aggressively, with an anger I've only ever seen in the movies. He spit all over me as he spoke through clenched teeth. "I am a park ranger. You disrespected me. You paid the kid more than me." He lowered me back down so my feet could touch the ground, but he kept one hand around me. I wanted to cry, but there was no way I was going to give him the satisfaction. I stared him in the eyes and didn't say a word. "Why do you disrespect me?" he said with foam collecting at the corners of his mouth. I said nothing. Part of me wanted to answer, hoping it would de-escalate the situation, but the other part wasn't sure I could talk without breaking down. I went into a place in my brain I've never been before. I tried to disassociate myself from my body in an attempt to not let him get to me. He squeezed my neck a little more forcefully with his one hand, shook his head at me and then stormed off, leaving me coughing and gasping for air.

It was a tough goodbye. I didn't want to tell Moses and Rupert what happened for fear Godfrey would find out and go after them too. I gave them both quick hugs and jumped into the bus, relieved to be out of there. I stayed composed the entire drive back to town, despite my heart racing and my body shaking from the trauma and anger I had.

I had one night at the hostel before I could leave Arusha and be completely certain I wouldn't see Godfrey. I felt ridiculous considering the idea that I'd see him again, until I heard a pounding on the door of my room. "I know you are here." It was Godfrey threatening me. I'd had to share some personal information, including my place of stay in Arusha, when I started the hike. That is likely how Godfrey found me. "Open the door," he demanded. It sounded like he might have been drinking. I didn't say a word. Instead, I quietly picked up the little table that was in the room and placed it in front of the door, along with the chair, my backpack and my body weight. I sat on the floor and listened to his anger escalate while he ruminated over Rupert's tip and the notion that I perceived a lowly cook to be more worthy than fantastic him. I didn't have a phone or another way out, so I simply waited until he got tired and left. It was surprising to me the length of time he stayed, but eventually he announced his departure with one final kick at the door. It would be the final jostle he'd ever give me.

EPILOGUE

◎ **MY FIRST FEW DAYS IN AFRICA** were anything but perfect. My instincts and judgment were challenged more in five days than likely my entire life previous. It wasn't the dreamy, once-in-a-lifetime experience everyone said it would be. It was uncomfortable, scary at times and eye-opening. Yet everything about it felt real and raw and exciting. In the end, I got everything I asked for: a physical and mental challenge. Perhaps the events didn't go the way I expected them to, but that was also part of the draw. I refused to let this experience set the tone for future trips. Instead, I intended to use the lessons I learned about altitude acclimatization, cultural nuances, listening to my gut instinct and having faith in my own ability to make better decisions later on. A few bad experiences were not going to deter me from seeing more of Africa. My mind was made up; this was just the beginning of many more mountains, mishaps and miracles to come.

UGANDA – BWINDI

THERE I WAS – face to face with a silverback gorilla deep in the Bwindi Impenetrable Forest of Uganda. He was the largest member of the troop, at around 400 pounds. His russet eyes, tucked under his strong brow bone, were laser-focused on the seven of us as he stood completely still just a short pitching wedge distance away. The other gorillas were even closer and had us surrounded. They were preoccupied, eating leaves, passing significant amounts of gas (no judgment) and picking bugs out of their hair. It was only the leader that appeared to have trust issues. He slowly began to move on all fours in our direction. I could feel the park ranger's hand squeeze my forearm in an effort to communicate, "Don't move, stay calm." One swipe of the silverback's hand could knock you out cold, or worse.

Gorillas are an endangered species only found in the Virunga Mountains between Democratic Republic of Congo, Uganda and Rwanda. At the time of my visit there were less than 800 remaining. When I arrived in the Bwindi Impenetrable Forest, one of the first questions I had for the park rangers was about its name. I thought perhaps it was a little overkill – "impenetrable"? Really? It seemed like an exaggeration. I should have known better. This was Africa after all; nothing ever seemed to be toned down. Four professional animal trackers, one park ranger and one guide escorted me into the mysterious forest in search of the mountain gorillas for a once-in-a-lifetime experience.

Initially, it seemed ridiculous for all of us to be carrying machetes; especially inexperienced me, since the trail we followed was wide with a very gradual incline. I had created the belief that this was a very touristy, indulgent activity and therefore would be a simple walk in the forest leading us to a troop of gorillas in captivity. In my mind anyone who was privileged to afford an excursion like this would walk on the same path, to the same gorillas, take virtually the same photos, and then leave to post them on Facebook. Even with my cynical attitude, I still had the curiosity to go. I was in the region anyway, so it seemed a shame to miss an opportunity to see the last remaining gorillas, just in case one day they tragically disappeared.

We walked for about an hour on the open trail and I anticipated we'd arrive at the "zoo" shortly. The park ranger and guide stayed with me while the gorilla trackers dispersed into the thick green vegetation around us. We walked another 30 minutes on the trail until a radio call came in to the guide. It was explained to me that the trackers had a clue for where to locate the gorillas. This was the first moment when I began to consider that perhaps this wasn't a "zoo" but rather a controlled nature park. I still wasn't convinced all of the walking wasn't for an "experience," and the machete, well I just thought that was ridiculous. *Look at this thing! What am I doing holding a giant knife?*

Then something happened. I was instructed to walk directly into the wall of vegetation to our right and slash whatever the heck was in front of us to pass through. I was like Indiana Jones (the clueless version). The park ranger followed behind the guide and me, rifle up at his chest in a ready position while we zigzagged up the side of the volcano whacking leaves, vines and branches in our path. The forest was so thick it blocked all sunlight, making it quite dark in areas, which was a contributing factor, along with the humidity, to its claustrophobic feeling. Without the machete it would have been nearly impossible to navigate some of the areas we ventured through. Some might have called it "impenetrable." Yes, that's me admitting I was ignorant. Luckily, my naive mindset did not convince me to ignore the attire recommendations I read online. Long sleeves and long pants were a must to protect your skin from the prickly thorns, sharp branches, mosquitos and other critters, which I chose not to think about. The constant hum of insects, laughter of the monkeys and various calls from the birds were a reminder of how much life we were surrounded by, even if we couldn't see them among the billons of leaves above, beside and below us.

Among the mingled noises we could hear the gorilla trackers' calls (a belching sound used to imitate how the gorillas communicate – their way of asking for acceptance) coming from above us. This was our notification that we were in the company of a gorilla troop. There was just one impressive obstacle between us: a nine-metre dirt wall that we would have to claw up. For safety, I was at the back of the pack this time in case we climbed to the top and found ourselves face to face with a gorilla. *Okay, this is getting real. You wouldn't do this at a zoo.* The soil and vegetation beneath us were soft and greasy due to the humidity. I grasped vines with my fingers and kicked my feet into the soil in a similar way to kicking my crampons into a glacier. The scenario felt much less safe, though, because we didn't have a harness and rope to rely on if we fell. About halfway up the embankment, the park ranger lost his footing but kept his handhold on a vine, causing his lower half to abruptly swing off the wall, accidentally kicking me in the face. Fortunately, he was able to continue to hang on, secure his feet again and prevent a long, tragic fall for both of us. My ear was ringing and I was uncertain whether it was blood or sweat dripping down my neck. Taking a hand off to check was not an easy option, so I just kept climbing.

The park ranger offered his hand when I made it to the top and dragged me up over the edge of the slick wall. Blood dripped onto the leaves beneath me, answering my burning question. But all was forgotten when I stood up to discover all four gorilla trackers standing in a line, looking curiously in one direction. Initially, it was like a *Where's Waldo?* scenario; I knew what I was looking for, but I couldn't see them. The crew kindly pointed my gaze in the right direction. At first glance all I could make out were what I thought to be dark crannies of the forest. But with further inspection it became apparent the black holes were actually 200-pound black-haired mammals nestled in the greenery. *Oh my word. This is WAY better than I expected.*

The trackers used their belching sounds to announce our presence and very slowly walked further toward the gorillas while the three of us followed. I was instructed before we left to make as little sound as possible, avoid eye contact with the gorillas, move very slowly and not to use flash photography. As a rule follower, and someone who wanted to avoid being mauled or trampled, I was very happy to comply. To avoid making destructive noise, we waded through the deep prickly brush without using our machetes, and unsuccessfully avoiding the low-hanging vines and leaves on the trees as they smacked us in the face on our way to a closer vantage point. It felt like the impenetrable forest was a natural protective barrier between gorilla and human. In a small way, it was comforting to know that at the very least this would make it more challenging for just any poacher to find them.

The guys continued to move forward, one foot at a time, slowly, slowly. I couldn't believe we kept going. If it had been up to me, I would have stood at the wall we just scaled! Instead, we tucked under a huge, low canopy of leaves in an attempt to camouflage ourselves just a few feet away from the giant mammals. The seven of us stood motionless, attempting to make as little noise as possible. It proved to be a very challenging task with all the pointy branches, ants and mosquitos attacking us. My whole body was one big itch I couldn't scratch.

The gorillas calmly sat in the grass picking branches off the trees with their thick fingers and nibbling the leaves off with their lips. *Uh uh uh* sounds were regularly made to communicate, "Back off, that's my branch!" We'd also hear singing periodically or a little chuckle from a member of the troop, indicating contentment. But if there was even one slight shift heard from our group, immediately they all went silent and we were glared upon. It was very clear our presence was known and we were simply being tolerated.

I cautiously took photos of the playful baby gorilla in the branches adjacent to the tree we were under. His wide, curious eyes paired with the soft-looking puffs of hair covering his body melted all of our hearts. He would beat his little chest when an older member was nearby, reminding me of a little boy flexing his biceps to show off for his dad. I could have easily watched him all day plucking single leaves off a branch, inspecting them, squeezing them into his little mouth and repeating until his eyes got heavy and he'd nap for a few minutes until he'd wake himself up with his own snoring. Repeat cycle.

The older gorillas had a similar routine, just with more aggression and a larger consumption of food. Periodically, they would play fight by grabbing one another's hair and yanking each other down to the ground. They'd roll around and groan or get distracted by a fly or a bird and forget what they were doing.

My nerves began to ease after observation that we were ignored for the most part. I hoped the gorillas could feel we were harmless. I brushed the hair off the side of my face and noticed I still had wet blood coming from somewhere. None of the guys said anything, so I was confident it wasn't anything bad. Then, out of nowhere, I felt a very small, specific point on my scalp start to burn. I tried to ignore it, thinking it would subside in a few minutes, but it didn't. It seemed to be worsening or even spreading; I couldn't quite tell. Initially, I linked it to the kick to my head, but as the pain increased I wondered if perhaps I was punctured by something sharp or a very thin ray of sun was beaming down and burning me. Unfortunately, I don't have any recollection of seeing the silverback gorilla crawl out of the forest into our view because all of this occurred while I was distressing over what was happening to my cranium. Eventually, I could decipher that the initial burn hadn't spread; there were just multiple new burns that were created. My entire scalp was on fire and I wanted to find out what the cause was, but I was too scared to talk standing in the company of eight goril-las within about 800 square feet of us. Tears welled in my eyes mostly out of worry but also terrible pain. My nose began to run and I sniffed as quietly as I could. The park ranger looked over at me, instantly granting forgiveness for the little sniffles and gulps I was making when he saw the distress on my face. I tilted my head down and pointed to it so he could look at what was happening. The unknown cause was terrifying and made my mind race with bad thoughts. *What if it's poisonous? What if it spreads even more? What if he doesn't find anything? What if this pain is permanent? What if...?* The ranger began to sift through my hair, eventually focusing his attention on a single area that I felt was one of the burning spots. He fidgeted around for a moment and then held something up between his thumb and index fin-ger to show us. He huddled in and whispered, "Stingy wasp." I was so relieved. *I'm not going to die! It's just a wasp. Damn, must be a powerful African variety, because I'm kind of hurting.* The pain was certainly not gone, but my imagination had been making it much worse than it was.

The trackers began to make their gulping sounds and the ranger pulled me in tight toward him. For the first time I noticed

the silverback. He was nearly twice the size of the other members of the troop, and he watched us with intensity, standing
strong on all fours. The trackers continued to communicate with
him to let him know we meant no harm, but he wasn't in the
mood for discussion. He sat up on two legs and showed his teeth,
then let out a blood curdling *WAAAAAH* sound. In a matter of
seconds, nearly 400 pounds of muscle and bone were charging
toward us. Even if we had time, there was absolutely no way we
could outrun him through the dense vegetation. Our only option
was to remain as still as possible and try not to irritate him any
more than we already had. He growled at the last second, just as
he veered off to the side of us, grazing two of the trackers. It was
a terrifying display of power and an indicator it was time to go!

Okay, definitely not a zoo.

The silverback trampled through the forest and circled back
just as we were leaving. The trackers and the ranger had their
guns up, ready to scare him if absolutely necessary. Luckily, that
wasn't the case, and we left with no more drama.

Not long into our walk back, the trackers parted ways. The
guide explained that we were no longer in typical gorilla territory. I used the opportunity to ask them to look at my head again
since it was still burning quite a bit. I'd been stung by wasps in
the past and never felt the pain spread to such a large area like
this. My concern was that I was having an allergic reaction.

Initially, only the ranger felt it necessary to inspect my head,
but when he gasped in horror the guide quickly joined in. It
turned out that several wasps were still stuck in my hair, but
not alive. The guide and ranger counted the welts on my head
and stopped after 12. "This is very stingy," the guide said with no
inflection in his voice, leaving me to decipher whether it was a
statement or a question. "Yes," was my safe polite response. But
in my head I was actually thinking, *It's friggin' stingy! My melon is
on fire right now and it's a lot of effort to stay this cool in front of you.*

Besides, I can't cry while holding this hard-core machete – that would offset the bad-assery I have going on right now.

We had one last steep section to climb to make it back onto the path we'd started on. This was not a vertical wall like the other, but it still required a crawling movement to prevent tipping backward. I followed behind, this time leaving a bit more room between the ranger and me. The slimy conditions resulted in another accidental slip, but this time the ranger was able to regain his footing thanks to the less severe incline. His rifle, on the other hand, reacted a bit more unfavourably. It was worn across his body and somehow slipped off his shoulder, down his back, the butt plate smashing me between the eyes. Once again, I was seeing stars and wondering about blood. We scrambled our way to the path and I assessed the damage with my fingers. No blood, but one impressive goose egg. *Well, that was something!*

Humbling is what it was. I left that day with one black eye, a head laceration, at least a dozen wasp stings resulting in enough inflammation to cause my hair to later fall out in those spots and a hematoma smack dab in the middle of my forehead. It wasn't an easy day, but it's also one of the most memorable in all my 43 years of life. I had the privilege of spending time with a few of the remaining mountain gorillas left on the planet – in the wild, not a zoo. I stand corrected. Once again, Africa kicked my butt and had me craving more.

KENYA

Approximately 6:00 a.m.

IT WAS GETTING BRIGHT ENOUGH to not need our headlamps any longer. We couldn't see it through the storm, but the sun was rising. The light provided a glimmer of hope that perhaps the sun would burn off the clouds and leave us with an opportunity to walk safely down the mountain. Samuel encouraged me to keep going with my storytelling, until we heard voices. "Did you hear that?" he asked with disbelief in his voice. "I did!" I replied, equally baffled. We both cautiously pulled the tinfoil blanket off our heads and stood up to look over the boulder that was sheltering us. The snow was still coming down fiercely and the wind was just as aggressive. To our disappointment, the visibility conditions had not improved one bit, even with more daylight.

From what felt like out of nowhere, two gentlemen stepped through the thick white wall of snow and approached the rock we were standing behind. I questioned whether I was dreaming or if I'd died. I was not an expert, but the conditions were so harsh it seemed impossible for another person to be up here, navigating safely. "Hey!" I yelled out over the wind. If I had not alerted them, they would have easily walked past without noticing. Our perch was a few feet below the path they were traversing, so both men looked down and to their right to see where the voice was coming from. "Hey, down here!" I yelled out one more time to direct them. Their eyes scanned around until they focused below their feet and caught a glimpse of my red coat. "Hello!" the gentleman in a fluorescent yellow rain suit and brightly coloured green rucksack said back with enthusiasm. He was clearly flabbergasted to see us too.

He and his guide carefully stepped down to where we were situated and briefly discussed their plans to continue back to the camp we had left earlier in the day. They had summited Mount Kenya in the early morning from the other approach, and it looked like the altitude and weather had taken their toll. The gentleman in yellow was from London and looked to be in his late 30s. He briefly mentioned this was his first trip to Africa and it was a dream to be hiking Mount Kenya. In spite of his visible fatigue, he talked with laboured breath about their trek up, the exhilaration he felt when summiting and how excited he was to email his family about his accomplishment. Samuel quickly spoke to the gentleman's guide in Swahili, which admittedly piqued my curiosity because there were only two topics they could be discussing: the weather and our safety. Those two knew a lot more about what were considered "normal" conditions for the mountain than me. It seemed like things were pretty bad, but I thought perhaps I was overreacting. I wanted to have their perspective. In the end, the British gentleman and his guide parted ways and decided to continue down to the camp, despite the extremely poor visibility. Samuel apologetically said he wanted to sit a bit longer before we walked anywhere. "I think it is not safe. The other guide does not believe me, so they will walk. I think we will wait."

I was cold and really didn't want to wait any longer, but I respected Samuel's decision. He didn't want this any more than I did, so he clearly felt it was the right choice to make. We ducked back down into our nook and held the blanket over our heads. "Where to next?" he asked with anticipation. "How about Ethiopia and then Morocco?" I asked back. "Yes, these are good places, I believe," he answered back positively.

ETHIOPIA

I SAT ON THE SMOOTH ROCK beneath me and hugged my knees to my chest. I felt so small and insignificant, yet so proud of myself for finally making it here. I did it.

I had seen pictures in travel books and read extensively about the region, but seeing it in person, watching the sunset behind it, was breathtaking and emotional. My eyes traced every line I could on the grand rock carving below the earth's surface. I was looking down on one of 11 underground churches hewn into the landscape of Lalibela. Almost my entire life, I had dreamt of this moment.

As a small child I was drawn to Ethiopia for reasons I do not fully know or understand. I was consumed with watching the 1980s famine telethons on TV, shocked by what tragic conditions people were enduring but inspired by their resilience, work ethic and community. The people of Ethiopia touched me in such a powerful way that my innocent childhood curiosity continued into my teenage years and transitioned into an obsession. I collected pictures and articles from magazines that had anything to do with Africa, but in particular, Ethiopia. It was at this time in my life I learned about the underground churches. I taped pictures of my favourite images to the inside cover of my daytimer. Every 12 months I would carefully remove them like they were the most precious things I owned and transfer them into my new one. I did this for nearly a decade, sometimes adding a new photo, never replacing one though.

My magazine clipping of Lalibela was always in the centre of the page, right from the beginning, emphasizing its importance. As a young adult in university my ambition to travel was at an all time high. I was so close to my dream, yet so far away. I didn't have the money to fly to Africa just then, so I lived vicariously through Ian Wright, host of the television show *Lonely Planet*. I can't be certain how many times I rented the tapes from the library, but I can recite several of them by heart – even using my very terrible English accent. Along with my adventure programs, I would escape by running – for hours and hours. I'm talking bat-shit-crazy level running. I would let my mind wander obsessively and travel in my head to some of the places taped inside my book. Within a few kilometres I could transport myself to the hills of Ethiopia, gently grazing my fingertips along the cool concrete of the churches and leaping from one rooftop to the next. It was a dream, okay! (I realize leaping onto UNESCO rooftops is frowned upon.)

Here I was in my early 30s, finally with the means to fly to Ethiopia and see, in the flesh, what I had dreamt of most of my life. The day was perfect and exceeded my own imagination – with the exception of not having the ability to leap like a superhero. I walked the entire afternoon analyzing and appreciating the medieval and post-medieval civilization. It was the off-season in Lalibela, so very few tourists were in the area. I was fortunate to have some alone time and several opportunities to sit, reflect and appreciate my journey to get to where I was.

When the last hint of sun descended beyond the green hills, I made my journey back to town to have a quiet dinner at a little place I had spotted earlier. Along the way I collected several persistent followers. As one of the only obvious tourists in the region, I became the sole target for interested children. Initially, it was harmless curiosity, but then their grabbing and yanking of my clothing, camera and arms escalated. It became an irritation and a disruption to my good mood. I held onto my camera tightly as the kids circled me in an attempt to take it. My last night in Ethiopia, and plans for one final authentic meal, were hijacked. The gang of kids around me had grown to at least 50 or more and they were becoming increasingly cheeky. Although they were just kids around the ages of 6 to 16, it was clear I could not underestimate them. I was outnumbered and it didn't feel safe. The kids were making it very clear they were about to do almost anything to snag my camera. I passed by the restaurant I had intended to enjoy and went straight back to my hostel instead. The kids followed me right to the entrance and then loitered outside while I took a moment to figure out what I would do for food. It was an eerie feeling to be the only person staying the night at the hostel. Most of the lights were turned off and there were no staff members to be found, with the exception of the gentleman at the door, thankfully keeping the kids at bay.

I went up the one flight of stairs to my room and dropped my camera off. I decided I'd go next door to the little cafe attached to the hostel and get a small bite to eat there. The kids were still outside the entrance when I walked out. Luckily, I only had a few feet to go. When I stepped inside, it appeared that the cafe was closed. A slender gentleman with crossed eyes walked out from the back and greeted me. "Hello, do you want some food?" he asked. "Yes, are you still open?" I inquired politely. "Yes, but we do not have very much to offer. It is because of the low season," he explained. "Anything will be fine," I said, hoping he could come up with something. "A cheese sandwich?" I suggested, thinking that might be a quick, easy option. "Yes. I can make one for you. It will take some time. Is this okay?" he asked. "That is fine. Thank you!" I said sincerely.

He didn't offer to explain why it would take some time to make a sandwich, but I assumed it was because there wasn't any food in the cafe. The entire place was empty, with the exception of a dirty cloth on the counter and a few tables and chairs. "How much do I owe you?" I asked, eager to pay. He took a while before he answered, as if he didn't really know. I assumed this was an indicator that cheese sandwiches were not on the menu, so he was making something up – which I was totally fine with. "One dollar," he responded. I put two dollars on the table and asked what time I should come back to pick it up. As I was asking I could see the crowd of kids outside the door watching my every move, waiting for me to walk back out onto the street. The gentleman could sense my discomfort with the attention. He promptly walked to the entrance and yelled at them to go away. They didn't leave, but at least they stepped back to the other side of the street to give me some breathing room to walk back to the hostel. "The kids will wait for you. It is better I bring you the sandwich. To your room, is this okay?" he asked generously. I was grateful and relieved for his offer. "Thank you so much. I appreciate that. I am in room number 9," I responded back. I was so relieved to be spared more harassment.

After almost three hours of waiting for my sandwich, I eventually tuckered out and fell asleep while reading my book. I was woken up by a gentle knock on the door. I was confused and had forgotten about the arrangements that were made. "Yes, who is it?" I asked with a little trepidation. "I have your sandwich, Miss," a familiar voice responded. Groggily, I opened up the door to discover the toothless gentleman from the cafe holding a plate with a terribly dry-looking sandwich on it. "Thank you so much," I said back, still a little out of it after the abrupt wakeup. I took the plate from his hands and then made a tragic mistake I will never do again. I turned my back to him to place the sandwich down on the desk. I wanted to free up my hands in order to offer him a tip for his kindness. When I turned back around my heart stopped momentarily with the discovery that he had welcomed himself into my room and closed the door behind him. *Oh my word. Shit! Shit! Shit!* was all I could think.

I didn't move. I didn't say anything. He began to shuffle toward me, eyes on mine the entire time. I slowly stepped backward, wanting to avoid his creepy eye contact but needing to pay close attention to his hands. He followed me and very quickly I ran out of real estate, discovering I was trapped between him and the wall.

"Your hair is so black," he said quietly, like he was trying to be sexy or something. I didn't respond. I was trying to get a gauge on what his intentions were exactly. He lifted up his hand to touch the side of my head and feel my hair. "It is soft," he continued. I tend to laugh or use humour when I'm in pain or scared. I think perhaps it might be my way of distracting myself or coping. I was pretty damn scared at this moment, which is likely the reason for my response: "I use Pert Plus. It's inexpensive. And I like green." *I like green? What is that?*

He kept petting me like a cat and my skin wanted to crawl off my bones. "Your teeth are so white. The opposite of your hair," he went on. *Well, at least I know I'm not dealing with a clever one here.* "You are so white. And so beautiful," he awkwardly said in his very non-sexy whisper. "Yes, I am very white. I'm also very hungry," I commented back. "Can I kiss you?" he asked bluntly. "No, you can't," was all I said. "I really want to kiss you," he pushed a little more. "Well, you can't," I said firmly. I tried to slide along the wall to get away from him, but he moved in even closer and tried to pull my head in toward his wet puckered lips. I pulled my head away and then shook it around like I was at some kind of headbanger concert, to get him off me. It totally worked! "Please let me kiss you. Just once," he begged while he attempted to stop my head from thrashing back and forth. "I love you!" he went on, sounding desperate. "You are my goddess." I continued to insanely swing my melon around in an effort to avoid his hands from trapping it again.

When he couldn't gain control of me he started to sob. A small part of me felt bad for the guy, but the other part was pretty certain he was manipulating me. I wasn't going to take any chances by showing any sign of sympathy or concern, despite that being my natural tendency. Instead, I used his sobbing as a way to get away from the wall. "Let's go sit down and talk," I said as calmly as I could. "Oh, okay," he said. "On the bed?" *What a rat! I knew it was an act!* My mind raced a mile a minute as we walked over to the bed. *Clearly, this guy is visually impaired, but I think he might have some kind of mental illness as well. I wonder how aggressive he could become? This wasn't in the* Lonely Planet *Ethiopia video! I'm going through all this for a gross-looking sandwich? It's not even toasted! How am I going to get out of this?*

"I can see you want to kiss me now," Mr. Sexy Pants said to me, through his sexy dinosaur tears. "No. I do not want to kiss you. I would like for you to leave now," I said directly. He slowly crumpled up like a newspaper, slid off the bed and sat on the floor like he was 5. *Well, that was a dramatic manoeuvre. I'm not sure he understands what is attractive to the ladies. Oh shit, he's petting my feet! My suspicious were correct, because anyone in his or her right mind with half-decent eyesight would NOT want to touch my heinous feet. Right now I have a crazy person on my hands...er, feet!* "You are my white goddess," he began again with the embarrassing comments. Kneeling over the edge of the bed, he began to kiss the tops of my big toes where there used to be nails. Did I mention I spent three weeks hiking in the Simien Mountains just before I visited the area? "Your toes are salty," he informed me. *I wonder if he finds puking ladies attractive?* I had him right where I wanted him. All I had to do was kick him hard enough; his face was right there!

There was only one problem: I didn't have the heart to do it. He was clearly unwell. Aggression would be my last resort option.

Yeah, I know what you're thinking: *This* wasn't your last-resort moment? (I know. I'm thinking the same thing while writing this.) "I'm really hungry and I'd like to have that cheese sandwich now. Would you mind giving me some time to do that?" I asked as nicely as I could while trying to pull my toe out of his mouth. He licked the top of my foot before he responded, "Yes, after one kiss." *This guy is as persistent as they come!* "I appreciate the sandwich and in return I already paid you for it. That is enough. I am *not* going to kiss you," I responded back, with a little more assertiveness (but not too much to piss him off). I still wasn't sure what he was capable of. I gently slipped my foot out from his hands and slowly stood up. It was obvious he wasn't going to leave if I didn't do something more. He kneeled down and started to cry again, kissing my feet profusely. *Not this again! Come on man, pull yourself together. This is not the touching moment I was hoping to have in Ethiopia.* It was pretty much the worst thing ever. I don't even like pedicures.

I shuffled sideways very slowly toward the door at the front of the room. My foot was leaving disgusting streaks of saliva along the wood from his fervent licking. I kept my eye on him the entire time until I backed myself up to the door handle. I was surprised and beyond relieved that he didn't do anything to stop me. He stood up and began to walk toward me with a different kind of look on his face this time. His once innocent desperate look was now one of frustration and anger. I grabbed the wooden chair that was tucked under the desk at the front of the room and threw it down between us to buy me time to open the door and run into the hallway. Just in case, I didn't stop there. I continued to run down the stairs and out into the dimly lit street to surround myself ironically with the kids that had previously irritated me. They immediately swarmed me like they had earlier, with intentions to pester a solo tourist for their own entertainment.

I became too overwhelmed with the attention and broke down. I crouched on the ground and began to cry out of frustration, but also relief for being out of the situation I had been in minutes ago. The kids stopped laughing and stepped back away from me to give me some space. "It's not you guys. I'm okay," I explained while trying to pull myself together. The group walked back and sat down on the road with me. A few of them patted me on the knee and rubbed my arms in an effort to console me. A young man put his hoodie over my shoulders and another shared his Coca-Cola.

This was the Ethiopia I had dreamt of. This was the Ethiopia I'd choose to remember.

The gentleman that was originally tending the door to the hostel caught a glimpse of me and walked over right away. "Miss, are you okay?" he asked, looking very worried. "Yes, I am okay. Thank you," I replied back, trying to keep myself together. I was still a little shaken up. "Did something happen?" he asked. I had mixed feelings about saying something. On one hand, I didn't want the mentally ill gentleman to lose his job, but on the other I also didn't want this to happen to anyone else. "I made a mistake. I should not have had the gentleman in the cafe bring me my sandwich," I said, trying to own the situation and protect him a little bit. "Did he do something?" he asked with alarm. "He let himself into my room. But I am okay," I said, trying to keep the tears from flooding my eyes. "Please, I don't think he is well. I don't want to get him in trouble." I followed up with, "I just think he should be kept busy, away from the ladies." The gentleman put his hand out to help me off the ground. "Let me escort you back to your room. I will make sure you are safe," he said kindly. He gave me the feeling this was not the first time he had heard this story. I thanked the group of kids for being so kind and slid the hoodie off my shoulders to return it to the young man. Before accepting it back, he leaned in and gave me a gentle hug.

When the two of us arrived back at my room, the gentle-man stood outside the door and asked me to look around to be sure nothing was taken. It hadn't even crossed my mind that my belongings might have been stolen. I immediately went to the bed and looked under the mattress; my passport and wallet were right where I'd left them. In fact, everything was. The only noticeable change: a bundle of bougainvillea flowers had been left on top of my backpack. It was either an apology or a sign he would be returning. "Miss?" The gentleman quietly checked in to see if I was okay. "Sorry. Yes, everything is here. Thank you so much for making me comfortable," I responded back. "Please, lock your door. I will sit at the end of the hallway to make sure he does not come back. You will be safe." He smiled warmly and closed the door for me. I did as he asked and tucked the wooden chair underneath the doorknob for a little extra security.

My first priority was to wash my feet! I knew it was going to be a sleepless night, so after I'd scrubbed the dried slobber off, I sat on the bed and nestled in for a long night of reading instead. Several hours in, beyond the pages of my book, I caught a glimpse of the cheese sandwich sitting on the desk across the room. *Don't even think about it. You can't eat that! What if he licked that too, before he brought it up? Even worse, what if he licked it after he licked your feet? You could get sick. It looks nasty.* Newspaper headlines ran through my mind: "Health Nut Killed in Ethiopia after Late Night Cheese Sandwich," "Carbs Kill Personal Trainer in Africa," "Late Night Munchies Take Their Toll on Fitness Fanatic," "Canadian Girl Loses Two Toenails and Her Mind in Ethiopia." The last one was the winner. I picked up the sandwich and devoured the whole damn thing.

MOROCCO

AFTER HOURS of casually exploring the maze of streets within the Marrakesh medina, I finally spotted what I was searching for. With sensory overload after weaving through crowds of people and market vendors, it was likely I passed several without noticing. Although it was tucked in the back corner of a narrow alley, in faded red paint, I could still make out the writing on the sign: Hammam.

"What is a Moroccan hammam?" I asked the first time someone insisted I try one. It was described to me as a communal bathhouse that is visited one to two times per week by most Moroccans. Many attend with friends or family to get help bathing hard to reach places (like your back), but it's also an opportunity to socialize and catch up on the day's events. I was assured when visiting alone that staff members would be present to direct me on what to do, and could help with the washing process.

Typically, going to a spa or relaxing of any kind is not something I gravitate toward, but the cultural experience I was promised piqued my curiosity. I'd been on the lookout for an "authentic" Moroccan hammam establishment all afternoon. The only guidance on selection I was given by the locals I met was to choose a place that looked "simple" not "fancy." This recommendation, albeit subjective, was intended to help me avoid Westernized, pampering versions. According to the locals

I met, it was a "must" that I experience a traditional hammam at least once. The spa-like versions were apparently very wonderful but different.

Navigating the dusty alley toward the wooden sign, I dodged a horse and buggy, a couple of erratic motorbikers and a group of women that smelled of lovely orange blossom. There were also several piles of rotting produce that smelled anything but lovely, and occupied the better portion of the walking real estate. Among the chaos, my attention was focused on the various items strewn on the street that I used as clues to determine if I was in tourist territory or in a local community. A hairbrush, a sardine can, a skirt, a crescent wrench, an empty bottle of olive oil and a hay bale were all indicators of regular, local life. I felt confident I was in "authentic" hammam territory, and that the establishment I was standing in front of would be suitable.

I tentatively unlatched the heavy wooden door to find a small entrance with nothing in it. As I looked around wondering if it was open, a woman casually walked into the barren concrete room from a side doorway, greeting me without a smile or pleasantry of any kind. *Egad! She's so scary!* With zero enthusiasm or expression, she blurted out aggressively, "Hammam?" *No! You're frightening!* "Ah, okay. Yes, hammam please." I replied back, against my own gut. *What was that? Why did you say yes?* I followed her nod toward the doorway she'd just come through. *Boy, she's a real chuckle. Hope she's not part of the bathing situation.* (Of course she was.)

I had the knowledge that I would be very clean after the hammam, but I had no additional information about the process or what to expect. After the experience, I documented the procedure in its sequential steps, which I will share with you now:

First, to note: I did not speak the language, so verbal communication was off limits. Squealing and grunting were not recognized as indicators I was in discomfort or pain and certainly not a reason for the procedure to take a pause or stop. It was also a huge disadvantage for question asking.

The play-by-play takes place immediately after I walk through the doorway into the next room with the unpleasant woman. I didn't catch her name, so I refer to her as "Chuckles." (I thought it was fitting.)

STEP 1: You walk into a floor-to-ceiling grey concrete room about 400 square feet in size. There is a drain that lines the perimeter, and an elevated rectangular concrete slab situated directly in the centre of the room. It's reminiscent of an Indiana Jones movie where the beautiful lady is almost sacrificed, or perhaps a slaughterhouse for cattle. The dungeon cell is the opposite of a spa. You want to tell all your Moroccan friends you found the least fancy place ever! *It's SO authentic. Who is a travel guru? You are!*

STEP 2: You are already questioning why on earth you said yes to this. Your heart is racing.

STEP 3: You bug your eyes out when you are given hand gestures indicating removal of all clothing – right here, right now. You are uncomfortable with this, but for some reason you do it. You can't put your finger on why, but perhaps it's the inviting atmosphere putting you at ease, or the awesome connection you've developed with Chuckles. While you fumble in compliance, the angry-looking woman stands with her arms crossed, watching you with immense judgment. You can't pinpoint what it is initially, but you sense she is irritated with something. Then it comes to you: everything. She is irritated with everything.

STEP 4: You question what is wrong with you for staying. You do not like this one bit, but your damn curiosity needs to know what is going to happen next.

STEP 5: You remove all of your clothing, with the exception of your underwear and bra. Chuckles expresses disapproval with an audible sigh and a roll of her eyes. She uses a violent hand gesture to communicate with you. You vacillate between two guesses for what she wants to say: "I will tear your bra off for you," or "I will rip you in half if you don't hurry up." Luckily, you are learning the language of terror that Chuckles speaks and frantically remove your bra before any unsolicited assistance can be offered. You make a mental note that being conservative is not an acceptable part of this process.

STEP 6: You mock yourself. *This is so authentic.*

STEP 7: You are completely naked now. Yup.

STEP 8: Chuckles grabs you by one arm and jerks you toward the sacrificial rectangle in the centre of the room. She pushes you down by the shoulders and forces you to sit on the concrete block. It is cold on your bare tuchus! Quickly you are nudged backward, indicating Chuckles wants you horizontal. Hesitantly, you lay supine on the firm slab, fully exposed and vulnerable to a very scary lady. *How could this get worse?* Chuckles yanks your feet apart like you're a rotisserie chicken and brings your hands over your head so you are now star-fished and at her mercy. She has a look in her eye suggesting she wants to put you on a salad.

STEP 9: You think to yourself, *after all this, I'm going vegetarian.*

STEP 10: *Splat!* A huge bucket of water is chucked over your fish-belly-white-naked self, without warning. It makes the concrete beneath you slippery and you slide sideways. Chuckles corrects this immediately by grabbing your left foot and swinging you back into position. You are impressed with her athletic manoeuvre.

STEP 11: The black soap comes out! You, of course, know nothing informative about this – what it's made of, its purpose or if you might be allergic. You don't dare request that Chuckles do a small test patch – that would be absurd. *You are like a local now. A travel guru!* Chuckles frantically spreads the black product across your stomach, down between your thighs, up and under your backside and all around your sensitive parts. There is black product in every nook and cranny of your body. If an allergic reaction is to occur, it will be a good one.

STEP 12: Abruptly, Chuckles leaves the room without any notice. You believe she needs to wash her hands after she rubbed hers all over you. You're confident she will be back, refreshed.

STEP 13: Chuckles does not return. You wonder if this is part of the process, or if it's lunchtime for her. You lay patiently, covered in black lather.

STEP 14: Chuckles is still not back and your black body is beginning to dry and harden. You wonder, *is this supposed to happen?* You lift your head slightly to look around, and the dried soap cracks around your neck. Your eyelids no longer move, so you survey through thin slits. The room is empty. This is somewhat of a relief knowing Chuckles is not lurking, watching you crisp to your death.

STEP 15: You give yourself a pep talk. *You're being dramatic. This is perfectly fine. You won't die from this. Remember, you're a travel guru! This is SUCH a cultural experience.*

STEP 16: You decide it's been long enough and you will now have to crack your lips apart to call for help. You think that one attempt will be enough, but to your surprise the black soap is mighty thick and it requires some decent effort to open your mouth. Once your lips are apart, you call out very timidly because you know you're in a pickle. You don't want someone else to come to your naked-black-soap-self rescue, but you also don't really want Chuckles to come back angry either. Your mouth doesn't move very well, so your *o*'s and *b*'s don't sound quite right. "Hellah? Any ody out there?" "Hellah?"

STEP 17: Nobody comes. You continue to wait patiently for you don't know what. So it becomes a time for reflection. After several minutes of pondering, you come to the realization that you've made a poor life choice. (Yes, indeed it is scary it took me that long for some perspective.) You spin the crummy situation in your mind to make the best of it, as you like to do. *Someone will find me eventually. There is nothing to worry about just yet. It's only been maybe 45 minutes? Be calm. What would Ian Wright do on the* Lonely Planet? *He'd battle, so you can too! This is so cultural. Heck, yeah! I'm in Morocco having an authentic hammam. Enjoy this moment. When is the next time you will ever get to just lie somewhere naked in public?*

That last part came out wrong. Anyway...

STEP 18: Chuckles storms back into the room without warning and begins to chuck buckets of water onto your face and body at a very rapid, scary and forceful rate. She moves so fast it makes you wonder if she is panicking that the black product has been left on too long. With every splash of water you feel like you're drowning. You spew water out of your mouth as quickly as you can between buckets, but it's tricky since your face muscles are still frozen in paste.

STEP 19: Chuckles is wasting no time now! She proceeds to scrub your skin with a very course brush with the same vigour as the water throwing. Your sunburned parts and regions that have never seen sunshine are being scraped with a force that feels far from pleasant. You are no expert, but you have suspicions that Chuckles left the black soap on too long.

STEP 20: Chuckles leaves the best for last and tackles your head. If rabid cats were to get caught in your hair, this would likely be a similar feeling. Strands are ripped out and you're almost certain your scalp is bleeding. You hit your breaking point. *Damn it, Ian would have made it all the way through!* You sit up and yell at Chuckles, "No!" and wave your hands back and forth, meanwhile noticing your nakedness. Of course, you know you're naked, but for some reason it's still a shock to see it again with your own eyes.

STEP 21: Chuckles stops all scrubbing and throws the brush aggressively to the floor. She has a smirk on her face that you can't quite read, but it makes you angry. She pulls you off the sacrificial block (which was an accurate name, in the end) and walks you toward the exit. You really want to hand gesture for a cover of some kind, but you don't dare, knowing it will piss Chuckles off. *Modesty is the enemy! Walk your buck-naked self into the next room and just hope you don't run into a family of five or something.*

STEP 22: You are relieved when you walk around the corner and don't have an audience. You are motioned to lie face down on the leather table next to the open fire. It's like a massage table but without a hole for your head. You lay your face sideways and fear for what will come next.

STEP 23: You think about what lessons will come from this experience. One that comes to mind quickly: don't do this again.

STEP 24: Sparks from the fire spit out onto your bare back and you are sure that your skin is now totally gone between this and the scrubbing prior.

STEP 25: What's the best solution for this? Hot oil poured all over your body, naturally. Your once clean arms, legs, tuchus and hair are now doused in argan oil. There is so much oil you no longer can stay still on the table. *Ah, there go the legs, sliding off!* You pull them back onto the table and then your shoulder goes over the opposite edge. It's a workout just to stay put. Chuckles swings you back and forth as she spreads the oil everywhere in her ever-so-calming way.

STEP 26: You think to yourself, *this is the worst massage in history.* The sparks from the fire spew out onto your exposed body and you decide you've had enough. Chuckles smirks again as you get up; apparently, this amuses her. You decide there is only one way to pay her back for her incredible service. Without warning, you give her a big, unexpected, oily, naked hug! *Take that, Chuckles!*

STEP 27: Chuckles nearly runs away, to your delight. You are beyond happy to discover your clothes sitting on a chair in the corner. (You were not excited about the prospect of wandering around the place to find them.) You slide your oily body into your pants and T-shirt, and tie your greasy hair back away from your face.

STEP 28: You leave the hammam establishment and negotiate the busy streets back to the riad you are staying at. Once again you discover all kinds of random items along the walk. This time, it's the treasures that stick to your exposed oily skin that catch your attention – like plastic bags, thread, newspaper and cigarette butts. You strut confidently like the true travel guru you are. You are oily, but you are rocking it! *I might not be Ian Wright...but I'm not Mrs. Wrong!*

Until a plastic bag flies up and sticks to your forehead.

EPILOGUE

◉ **I RECENTLY WENT BACK TO MOROCCO** and shared my experience with a local Moroccan friend of mine. He was shocked by my story and asked what crazy establishment I went to. So everything you just read has been suggested as being very poor customer service, and not typical. So please don't let my story deter you from trying this yourself.

KENYA

Approximately 7:30 a.m.

THE SNOWSTORM HAD EASED and left a deep layer of white slush across Mount Kenya. The temperature was still well below freezing, and my body was aching from being crunched up and chilled for hours. Samuel surveyed the area. Although the visibility wasn't excellent, it was possible to see the direction we needed to take toward the summit. "The summit is that way, Anyela," Samuel pointed out. "Do you think we can make it?" I asked with surprise and hopeful delight. "Yes, I think it will be God's wish," he said with happiness in his voice, wanting to please me.

We swung our bags on our backs and very slowly stepped out of the slippery recess in the rock and headed up toward the path. The snow accumulation was now calf-deep, so I continued to step into each of Samuel's footprints for energy conservation and security. The cliff was now visible and closer than I imagined. The approach to the top was dramatic. To our left was a crater lake that was completely covered in ice and snow. You could see the outline of it and appreciate its size even from a kilometre above. The blizzard had returned just around the time we made it to the sign marking our final elevation at 4985 m. Samuel and I snapped a few pictures but took very little time to appreciate the accomplishment. By that time, the snow had escalated to a level where there was no longer a view again. We both understood that the weather was not in our favour and things were about to get even worse, at least at the elevation we were at. Rather than hike traditionally down the mountain, we essentially slid in our boots like we were on skis along the other side of Mount Kenya. It was easier on the legs, and a little less mentally tiresome attempting to decipher between which rock surface was secure and which one would slip underneath you and cause a tumble down the steep mountainside. As we lost elevation, I lost tension in my body and gained appreciation for my life and for great people like Samuel. I believe if I had been up on Mount Kenya with any other guide we probably wouldn't have made it. Samuel's expertise and gut instinct saved us both that day.

Tucked down at the bottom of the valley was a small refuge, which Samuel pointed out when we were about a kilometre away. Our descent began in blizzard conditions and slowly transitioned to rain. The rocks were very slippery, but less so than the soil between them. We strategically leapt from one large rock to the next in the direction of the refuge. The rain poured down the hood of my coat in a consistent stream, making it impossible to lift my head up without getting water inside. It felt like someone was holding a garden hose over me. Both Samuel and I had holes in our boots, leaving our feet soaked and freezing. It made the tediousness of testing each surface before we stepped uncomfortable and mentally exhausting. Samuel would let out the odd *humph* in frustration. I couldn't blame him. The last kilometre of our day felt like an eternity. "Anyela, where to next?" Samuel hollered out over the sound of the smacking rain. "You want another story? *Now*?" I asked with surprise, lifting my head and allowing a surge of rain to splash on the front of my neck, down toward my chest and eventually over my stomach. "Please. I need a break," he explained. "Okay. I'll take us somewhere warm this time!" I said positively, trying to lift his spirits. "We're going to start in Zanzibar and then head over to Rwanda."

ZANZIBAR

HEY, **THE TRIP ISN'T OVER YET!** *Resist the temptation to write a sequential to-do list and enjoy the last hours here while you can,* I internally coached myself. There were five hours left before my flight would depart Africa. The commute from the little villa I was staying at was only about 90 minutes, but the cool, go-with-the-flow travel version of me was already being replaced with the responsible, orderly one. The latter version caused me to catch a taxi early, just in case there were any hiccups en route to the airport. I was coming to terms with the idea that my adventure had come to an end and I would be back home shortly with routines, calendars and too many plans for my liking. Unless there was some epic problem with my flight home, I didn't anticipate anything increasing my heart rate or raising the hair on my arms in the remaining time I had left. One part of me wished I could continue to live forever in the carefree adventurous manner I had during the past four weeks – the other part thought it would make it less special if I did. I'm thankful everyday that I have had the ability and freedom to live in both worlds, even for brief snapshots of time.

A taxi driver in an unmarked car pulled through the gate of the quaint, six-cabana villa I was staying at. The driver was in his early 20s, wore a size small T-shirt over size large arms, accentuating his pecs and biceps. I'm not sure if fitness fanatics are more likely to notice other fitness fanatics because they have an appreciation for the work that is required, or if everyone notices. Regardless, it was obvious to me this dude had been lifting some heavy things. He kept his bedazzled sunglasses low on his nose so he could make eye contact with unobstructed eyes and gave me a cool half-smile. He was efficient, spoke almost no English and seemed to be in a big rush to get going. I liked his go-getter energy! He yanked my backpack off my shoulder, pointed to the car indicating which side to get in and swung my bag into the trunk, which was secured down with a flimsy rope.

I gladly jumped in the front passenger seat as he offered. Sitting up there makes the ride more enjoyable to spark up conversation, if the mood strikes. Some of the most interesting conversations I've ever had have been in taxis. It's a great way to learn about a country, its culture, and, if you're really fortunate, to meet someone open to sharing a few good stories. I love to observe the similarities between people across the globe and to make out the differences in opinion and perspective. In my experience, the two most common topics that come up are love (or the lack thereof), and money (or the lack thereof). I've gained so much appreciation for life, not because of mountain climbing and the hard struggles to summit, but from the bits in between the climbs, sharing personal experiences and thoughts with strangers and then having their stories and vulnerabilities reciprocated from a different perspective. Depending on the destination, I have spent a few hours to a few days with the same individual as we've driven together. These times aren't filled with adrenaline or heart-pumping physicality, but it's these moments I often think of first when I look back on my time in a particular country.

The journey to the Abeid Amani Karume International Airport in Zanzibar was no exception.

Kwame, the driver, ejected his cassette tape and left us to commute in silence. I asked with hand gestures if I could roll down the car window and he responded with a thumbs up and another cool half-grin. The hot wind whipped my hair back and forth across my face as I gathered landmark information to be sure we were driving in the right direction to the airport. Twenty minutes into the drive and I was spotting familiar buildings and signs I'd seen from the initial commute to the villa four days ago. This gave me relief. I don't enjoy feeling like I have to verify every turn a driver makes, but when I travel alone I try to pay attention to my surroundings, at least a little bit just to be sure I'm not taken for a different kind of ride.

Once I was feeling at ease about our direction, I attempted to spark up a conversation. "Kwame, could we listen to your music?" I asked, politely pointing to the cassette tape, hoping he'd understand what I was asking. His eyes widened above his glasses as he drew them down his nose for me to see as he replied, "Yes. You like it?" He understood my request and slid the cassette tape back in and entertained both of us with a random mix of '90s rap and '80s power ballads. *This is awesome! He has Bon Jovi and Snoop Dogg!* We listened to the old-school playlist for about 45 minutes, exchanging smiles and making the odd shoulder shimmy here and there (okay, only I did that). Kwame would periodically punch me in the shoulder gently or squeeze my upper arm. I didn't think anything of it, I just assumed it was a way to connect since we couldn't really converse with our language barrier. I interpreted it as a "Hey, you're a total nerd, but I think you're all right."

Just as my guard had come down, he pulled off the main highway and headed along a red clay road. My shimmy went stiff immediately, even though Tupac continued to repeat "California" over the speaker. I nervously checked in with Kwame: "Short-cut?" I was desperately hoping he had miraculously learned English in the past five seconds and could confirm that indeed this was a really quick way to the airport.

Everything is fine – totally fine – absolutely fine, Ang. Nobody here is trying to hurt you. You're cool. It's just a little detour. I tried to talk myself out of a spaz. *You're cool. Just wait it out and see what this is all about. This is a little exciting.* Kwame kept me guessing by responding with another cheeky grin. It was the first time he did this without lowering his sunglasses, which freaked me out because I couldn't get a read on him. Two, three, 16 – heck, I had no idea how many minutes had passed. All I did know was that I was reaching panic mode with every one.

He looks really strong, but maybe it's a tight shirt illusion? His legs don't look particularly long. Maybe I can outrun him? How many kilometres have we driven off the main highway? I might not be fast enough, but perhaps I'll be able to kick him off me once he catches me. Then I think I can outrun him over a long distance. If I can make it back to the highway, I should be safe. The highway is busy and someone will surely help me. I've got plenty of time to catch my flight. Good thing I left early so I can run for my life. Damn it, I'm wearing flip-flops!

The conversation I was having with myself inside my head was all over the place and certainly wasn't helpful in easing my nerves. I had no concept of time, but it felt like at least a half hour had passed before Kwame finally turned off the road, into what looked like a driveway. I noticed that Tupac was still rapping "California," so it wasn't nearly as long as I thought it was. *What an overreactor! The song isn't even over. Pull yourself together, Angela. Don't jump to conclusions! Sometimes taxi divers drive off the road to who knows where. This is fine.*

The car rolled to a stop and Kwame turned to look at me. Once again he didn't lower his sunglasses. *Uh-oh. What's happening here?* I had conjured up the idea that all communication through sunglassed eyes was now potentially deceitful. "My home," Kwame said. His announcement didn't make me feel better. *What are we doing here? Dude, I need to go to the airport.*

Did we have some kind of miscommunication? Ha! Not funny. It's too early for joking like that. Typically, I'd be thrilled to visit someone's residence, but in this case I had a wee bit of trepidation because I DIDN'T KNOW THIS GUY! *Stay calm. Stay calm. Sure, we've had no lead-up discussion about this detour, and I can't see a reason for it, but I'm sure it's nothing. Maybe he just forgot his lunch? Yeah, it's probably that.* "Why are we here?" I asked with a little squeak in my voice. *He doesn't speak English you bonehead. And what was with that squeaky voice? Come on! That had absolutely no badass quality to it whatsoever. Harness your inner Tupac, lady! Surely, you've just given him further confidence he can tie you into a bow and leave you in the middle of this small farm.*

"Let's go," Kwame directed as he nodded his head to the side, indicating our direction. Scientists suggest that most of our communication is nonverbal. I remind myself of this constantly when travelling alone in a country where I do not speak the language. I pay attention to the details as much as I can and interpret them how I want to. Yes, so basically I'm just guessing the whole time. It's super science-y. The head nod gave me something to narrow in on, to ponder and take my focus off the anxiety I was feeling. My mind was working in overdrive to look for self-preserving positive signs. I came to the quick conclusion that a killer wouldn't nod his or her head; they would just grab you. *Obviously.* A nod is what a buddy would do. It's a casual, friendly gesture to point with one's noggin to indicate direction. Am I right? (Just say yes.) Hey, let's head to that coffee shop (insert head nod). Hey, look (head nod), that farmer's market vendor has the peas you want. (Head nod), let's shoot hoops over there! All of these examples work splendidly and in no way indicate a bad situation. "We will go" (so I can steal your belongings and leave you to die, later to be eaten up by Zanzibar insects) (head nod). See, this one doesn't work. Clearly, my amazing logic was making it obvious that Kwame's one small move was an indicator of friendliness not freakiness.

Even after my incredibly reliable analysis, I was still several percentages on the I-Shouldn't-Do-This scale. But, of course, I got out of the car and followed Kwame anyway, just as he requested. My internal dialogue was still working on all cylinders. *Everything is going to be all right, Ang. He nodded. It's a good sign – a friendly sign. He hasn't done anything to indicate that he's a violent or bad guy.* As we walked through the common area between four thatched-roof mud homes, I slipped both my flip-flops off and walked in my bare feet in case I needed to run. I decided in the car I'd be faster barefoot than in sandals. As we continued to walk through the small village, I scanned for other people. Each home had a colourful fabric door that lightly fluttered with the breeze. The calming feeling they provided was in direct competition with my escalating heartbeats. There were no signs of other family members. We were here alone.

I wasn't sure if that was better or worse.

The hard-packed earth beneath my feet was hot from the sun and it was burning my skin a little bit. I was resisting the urge to put my flip-flops back on. We walked behind one of the homes and found ourselves tucked between a mud wall and a row of trees, providing refreshing shade. Kwame stood next to me and put his hand around my upper arm and squeezed. This squeeze was different than the ones he used in the car. There was more force, more purpose behind it. *This is it. I'm going to have to fight him.* Ha! Even the thought was ridiculous. I hoped those years of watching the Ultimate Fighting Championship (UFC) would have taught me something. I was mentally preparing for a spastic exchange of physical blows. I had no clue how to fight. I'd try "UFC-ing" first, and if that didn't go well, I'd run. That was my plan.

With a bit of excitement, Kwame continued to grip my arm and tug me forward just far enough that we could see what was hiding in the shadows of the trees. I focused on what was in front of me, and then looked up at Kwame with a plethora of questions swarming in my head. I'm sure my eyes looked shocked and my mouth was wide open. His nonverbal response to my reaction was priceless. A huge toothy smile formed as he lowered his glasses down his nose, lifted both his arms up and flexed his massive pythons.

He'd brought me to his home to showcase his gym!

All along I was right. I was going to die. It would just be in a different way than I imagined – the good way!

Guilt and shame for thinking he might wear my skin as a hat consumed me. I was a grade-A jerk! Kwame picked up each barbell and pointed out the different materials he used to make them. It looked like two empty paint pails had been filled with mud or cement, or a combination of both, and were attached with a long wooden stick. Clearly, this was for deadlifting and squatting. He had another bar that was a bit shorter that he used to perform an overhead press and bicep curls. Next to the barbells was a tree that had a section carved out for pull-ups. Along with the barbells, Kwame had made dumbbells using what looked like the same materials. I switched from feeling horrified to honoured once I realized I'd been taken on a trip to see what Kwame so proudly created. I may have lost weeks of my life due to the stress in getting there, but the unexpected detour was worth it.

I pointed to myself and then to the barbells to politely ask permission to try them out. He nodded and gave me another thumbs up. The first one I picked up felt like it was about 50 pounds. The second one I could barely lift off the ground and it had bloodstains on the wood. (Apparently, I wasn't the only one that found it harsh.) Kwame took off his shirt and sunglasses and gave me a look I've seen thousands of times on the faces of the fellas at my gym – it was go time! The two of us coordinated our exercise sets around the available equipment, just like what I'd do at home. Deadlifts, squats, push-ups, pull-ups, overhead presses and groans. It was so much fun! Similar to conversations about love and money, weightlifting is universal. Most of the exercises we performed were the same, as was our appreciation for the discomfort. We didn't say a word in the time we were there, but it was the best interaction I'd had all month in Africa.

Kwame poured some water over my head, and then his, to cool off. We got back into the car a little wet and finished the last leg of our journey to the airport. By the time we arrived, I was dry and my arms were jelly. I felt fantastic and so happy for the experience. Kwame hauled my backpack out of the trunk and I quickly fished through the top pocket to find the exercise bands I travelled with. I handed them to Kwame as a thank you gift. He opened the bag and laced the green one around his shorts like a belt.

Time was actually now running out, but I couldn't leave without performing a few exercise demonstrations so he'd have ideas on how to incorporate them into his regimen. In the middle of the small airport parking lot he practised the movements with a few grimaces on his face, which delighted me. I was happy he'd be challenged with them. Challenge leads to change, and every fitness enthusiast, in any part of the world, appreciates that. He gave me another bicep squeeze and gently punched me in the shoulder one last time. I slung my bag onto my back and gently nudged him back, awkwardly. *Yeah, you can't compete with his level of cool, Ang. Just go. Leave before you embarrass yourself.*

I made my way toward the airport building and couldn't resist turning around for a final wave goodbye. (I know; I'm shaking my head too. Zero game.) Kwame waved back, lowered his sunglasses and winked once more. The green band was still around his waist. Somehow, he pulled that off and made it look really good. I wonder if he ever used it to exercise, or perhaps he simply started a new fashion trend.

RWANDA

SITUATED IN THE VIRUNGA MOUNTAINS located in Rwanda, bordering Uganda and the Democratic Republic of Congo, there I was. The chain of volcanoes consists of eight climbable peaks all over 3000 metres in elevation. It's remote, picturesque and with every turn it feels like a new adventure awaits. In all my travels, despite the risks, it is still my favourite place on the planet.

Dense green vegetation and mysterious fog enveloped the undulating peaks and valleys that made the area feel ominous and somewhat uninviting the day I arrived. It was fitting because just beyond the trees were the last remaining mountain gorillas, and a dangerous rebel group known as the M23s. I knew I had no business being there, but my absurd desire to finish what I'd started ultimately brought me back to this mysterious place for a second time. I had summited seven of the eight volcanoes on a prior trip and ran out of time to complete the final one: the highest being Mount Karisimbi, standing at 4507 m. There was unrest in the area the first time I had ventured to the region, but this time the war crimes activity was at an all time high. Kidnapping, rape, executions and forced recruitment of children were just a few of the atrocities occurring on a regular basis. The Government of Canada travel advisory specifically stated on its website to avoid all travel to the area due to the current political and security situation.

The government explained: "Avoid all travel" as it is "an extreme risk to your personal safety and security. You should not travel to this country, territory or region. If you are already in the country, territory or region, you should consider leaving if it is safe to do so."

Yet there I was, all by my lonesome with a simple backpack, a few snacks, a one-track mind, an overly optimistic (some might say delusional) mindset and a relentless passion for the road less travelled. That sentence could be distilled down to one word: bonehead. Yes, I was/am a bonehead. Please, follow along to find out just how much of one I really am.

I hired a local gentleman to drive me to the village nearest the trailhead of Karisimbi. The road was carved into the side of the volcano and it was questionable whether it was fit for a vehicle to drive on. Rutty red clay with frequent potholes big enough to swallow a small child made it slow going and extremely hard on the Toyota we were in. The gentleman driving had impressive skills, though, and a good sense of humour. "This is an African massage," he would say as my head hit the headrest repeatedly.

Upon arrival, I found myself in a community high up in the mountains consisting of more goats than people. I collected my bag, hopped out of the SUV and proceeded in the direction that was indicated by the driver. I had no clue where I was or what I was looking for. I walked through the village, hoping to see a sign or meet someone that could guide me. There were no indications this was even a hiking destination. The few locals in the area stopped everything they were doing and watched me with curious eyes. It was like they'd never seen a bonehead before. Random goats bumped into me while children waved shyly and giggled cutely when I returned the gesture. I meandered around a small grouping of clay huts, trying not to intrude while I looked for something that read "Karisimbi" or "Virunga Hiking." I was clueless!

Eventually, a gentleman about my age approached me without saying a word and handed me a small black plastic bag filled with something heavier than I expected. I had no idea who he was or what I was doing holding his little satchel. Unfortunately, I didn't speak the language and he didn't speak English, so I couldn't ask important questions like "What's in the bag? or "Who are you?" or "Am I in the right place?" He gave me a head nod to follow him, so naturally I did. That seemed like the safe, obvious response. Am I right or am I right? In my defense, the military jacket he wore gave me a hint of confidence that he was a trekking guide. I'd seen this formal jacket worn by rangers on my previous trip.

It was a big surprise to me that the head nod was an invitation to walk for just over an hour together. Is it just my interpretation, or does a head nod indicate more of a small walk or a-few-steps-over-here kind of scenario, not hours? Despite my misread, I continued to just put one foot in front of the other like a sheep would. I could have been walking to my death for all I knew.

We eventually made a brief stop at a small village hut where a young boy ran out to greet my leader. He handed him a bag packed for hiking; it was the reassurance I needed. I took the opportunity to formally shake my leader's hand in an attempt to be friendly. He squeezed it reluctantly, and did not smile or show any facial expression whatsoever while he did so. *Okie dokie. I guess it will be an extra quiet hike.* He was intense, lacked pleasantries (so I never did get his name) and was seriously intimidating. I didn't get the impression he was a mean guy, though. It felt more like he just took his job very seriously. It didn't feel the same as the Godfrey situation back on Kilimanjaro.

Once he had his bag on his back, the two of us walked at a very brisk pace further uphill through a couple more villages. At one point, four children enthusiastically ran out to greet us. I waved while my guide gently patted one of the young kids on the head as we went by. It was a little moment I needed that provided me peace of mind that the stranger I'd just met a few hours ago wasn't a psychopath. Psychopaths don't kindly pat small kids on the head, right? I had no phone to Google the answer, so I continued to follow him, trusting he wasn't going to let a water buffalo, gorilla or angry rebel attack me. All my trust was created from that one simple act. Yup, that's what boneheads do!

Another hour of militant walking through the thick forest passed. We were no longer within range of a village or civilization at that point. It was in this area that Dian Fossey's cabin was built when she was studying the gorillas.

My mind pondered what it must have been like for Dian to live in this region and to interact with the gorillas. Her conservation work would have been so rewarding and is needed even more than ever as the gorilla population is dwindling at an alarming rate.

I thought about Dian's legacy and momentarily let my mind wander away from focusing on what was beyond the trees surrounding me. Within minutes, multiple men in full military gear and armed with guns stepped out from the foliage onto the trail we were navigating. In total, there were ten of them. Yeah, *ten*. I had no idea if they were "good guys" or "bad guys." I was nearly shitting my pants but couldn't ask any questions, so I had a conversation in my head instead to keep myself calm. *Uh, hello? Do yah not think I might want to know what's going on here fellas? Anyone? Does anyone want to fill me in? I don't want to make a big deal out of it, but what are your plans for those hefty guns?*

My guide was expressionless and didn't acknowledge them, so I took that as a good sign and used it to find some perspective. *Everything is cool. Nobody looks particularly scared...except for you. Pull yourself together, Ang. If they wanted to shoot you, they would have by now.* It was so interesting; nobody said a simple *jambo/* hello or anything. Everything felt very organized and efficient, so perhaps that was the reason for the lack of communication.

As a pack, our pace picked up even faster and I found myself in the middle of what felt like a military training camp. This was the first time I had to work hard to keep up the same pace as my guide. *Geez! This guy is a Ricky Racer.* I'd met my hiking match!

The armed men walked around us in a large circular pattern, leaping over rocks, navigating trees and hacking down vegetation with machetes every so often to create a clearing. At all times they had their guns forward and ready. After a little panic I came to my senses when it became obvious that these gentleman were here for our protection. But the fact that there were so many made it very real just how dangerous it was to be in this part of the world. This is where boneheads like to vacation!

Hours later we arrived at what I thought was our campsite. I began to remove my bag off my shoulders. The guide shook his head in annoyance and then aggressively pulled it back up for me. Once again, it didn't feel like he was being rude; it was more of a language barrier/urgency situation. I'm not sure if our safety was in danger there or if he simply didn't want to delay our progress. Either way, it was very clear there was a reason behind our speed. So I just jogged along, doing my best not to hold the troops up. I talked to myself in my head to overpower the tense energy around me in efforts to keep things fun and positive in my own little world. *Alrighty then, I wonder what they would do if I stopped to take a selfie? I bet they'd lose it! I wonder what these fellas are like after a few beers. I bet the one with the backward hat is a hoot!*

Our elevation gain was already over 2500 m, which is a significant climb in terms of altitude. The cardinal rule for trekking a mountain is to go slowly in order to acclimatize appropriately. Moses taught me that lesson on Kilimanjaro. We were not abiding by this rule. Instead, the 12 of us continued up the volcano at a very steady, quick pace. Okay, it was almost a run. We hadn't eaten anything or even sipped a drip of water. I was in the company of machines, making it almost impossible to even hand signal for a hydration break. I thanked my lucky stars that my dehydration left me with no need to pee. I could only imagine how irritated that would have made the fellas! *Who in the world stops to pee? Only wimps pee. I'm so strong I haven't peed in 12 hours!*

I knew my ego was getting in the way of my safety. It's another classic bonehead move. My body was tuckered, but I felt an unnatural desire to keep pushing at the uncomfortable pace to see how long I could do it. For that, I needed to enlist my best distraction weapon: Salt-N-Pepa! I quietly sang "Shoop," except in my modified version it wasn't men that were my weakness. More like my legs and knees. As you can imagine, this ditty put a jump back in my step and I was flying up the volcano. (Not really, but that would have been awesome.)

The sun was starting to set as we raced through the gnarled mossy trees toward Karisimbi's peak. At some point between the camp and the summit I realized I was still holding the mysterious black baggie of goodies. The trek was so intense I didn't even realize it. I hastily set the baggie down and took two pictures of myself at the sign marking the summit at 4507 m. Thick white fog surrounded us, making it an anti-climactic view. This, of course, didn't bother me one single bit. The journey and the push were what I wanted, and I certainly wasn't feeling deprived of exertion. The fellas kicked my tuchus! A common recommendation for acclimatization when you are above 3000 metres is to not exceed more than 300 metres of additional elevation gain a day. If you do, you risk altitude sickness of varying degrees. I was in awe that all 12 of us completed the entire trek (about 2000 metres) in hours, not days, and nobody seemed to be affected by it. Luck was on our side – or at least mine. My legs, on the other hand, were wobblier than normal heading back down. They had certainly been given an epic workout and they still had their work cut out for them. There was no easing down the volcano back to camp. It was a run. My legs were ticked off and wanted to disown my body.

Upon our arrival at our camp, the moon had replaced the sun. I hesitantly pulled my bag off my shoulders, hoping it was okay this time. If it wasn't, I'm sure I would have had to show my cards and admit I was an imposter crew member. There was no way I could keep our pace any longer. My guide nodded with approval while my quads, feet and ego said thank you. *Oh my word, thank you!* Before I set up my tent I had a peanut butter sandwich and all of my water: the first gulps of the day. It felt like the water was plumping my skin back up as I drank it, while the peanut butter filled my soul with energy and delight. It was an amazing sandwich. A-maz-ing.

We didn't have a fire that evening, which I suspected was due to a safety protocol. Fire draws attention and we were avoiding that, being right in the heart of M23 rebel territory. There was uneasiness in the air. Nobody said a word to one another while they set up camp and prepared their meals very quietly. I wasn't quite sure if it was 100 per cent for our safety or if the fellas were also just not into talking.

There was no reason to stay up, and I was unbelievably exhausted (in a joyous way), so I went to crawl into my tent. A good night rest was my only hope for being able to run again the next day. I was alarmed to see that five of the ten men were strategically sitting around the outside perimeter of my tiny shelter. The other five sat around the perimeter of my guide's tent. They had their guns pointing outward, ready if necessary. I've never seen anything like it. I crawled into the front door and zipped myself in. It was unsettling yet oddly comforting to know how many armed men were literally just on the other side of the nylon that surrounded me. I think this would typically result in a very poor sleep, but for a bonehead it was of no consequence. I slept like a cat on a lap.

When I stepped out of my tent early the next morning, the sun was just making its way up and there were still five fellas on guard. I had a situation. *How is a gal supposed to pee and be discreet about it?* I tried to ask with hand gestures (picture that for a moment, will yah?) That was just embarrassing and wasn't going anywhere. So instead I ventured innocently into the forest for some privacy. Three men immediately followed me and formed a circle, backs respectfully toward me in an effort to create a human outhouse. This took the meaning of gun-shy to a whole new level! I crouched down, trying so hard to do my deed, but nothing would happen. One of the men slightly turned his head to check on me without trying to see my pasty buttocks. *Yeah, I'm trying dude. Sorry! I want this to end just as much as you do – probably even more!* The pressure to get things flowing was stunting me. My legs were angry from the day prior and the long squat wasn't helping them. We all waited, and waited, and waited. Have ever you tried to pee with three armed strangers around you? *I'm working on it fellas. Give me a break!* Finally, after too much time, my body let it go. The three men tapped the ends of their guns on the ground quietly in celebration. I'm certain my cheeks (not those cheeks!) went red. It was the first and only emotion they showed the entire trip. At least now I knew they were human.

There was no time spent having coffee, eating a fancy breakfast or chatting about our feelings that morning. I took down my tent, scarfed down a dry bun and started the descent with the troops in full-tilt mode. It appeared I was the only one that had tired legs. Show-offs.

After hours of running down the volcano, I recognized Dian's cabin to our left. This was an indicator we only had a short distance left to travel. Just as the ten gentlemen mysteriously appeared, they vanished while I was admiring Dian's lodging. There was no opportunity to say thank you, or to even shake hands. It felt like the Virunga version of *Field of Dreams* when the baseball players slowly, one by one, disappeared into the corn-field. With one head turn, they were gone.

Another hour later we arrived back to my guide's village and stopped at the same place we originally met. He didn't say a single word. Instead, he tapped my shoulder as if to say "you" and then gave me a thumbs up. I'm not sure what he was try-ing to say exactly, but it seemed like it was something okay. I handed him an envelope for payment and gave him his little black satchel back. A wee smile of surprise invaded his lips as he gently took the baggie in his hands and inspected the contents inside. It was eggs! All that time I had been carrying food to eat along the way and didn't know it. He cracked the shell off of one and handed it to me to eat. I've eaten a lot of eggs in my time, but that one had to have been one of the worst. You'd think with how hungry I was it would have been delicious, but instead it tasted a lot like inevitable food poisoning. When I was finished, he handed me a second and, of course, I accepted – because I'm a bonehead! Luckily, my ride came just in time so I could get out of eating a third. My body was shocked by what had happened to it, and my mind was equally in awe of the happenings. The entire experience felt like a dream until about one hour into the bumpy ride back when the eggs reminded me it wasn't.

EPILOGUE

◎ **TO THIS DAY** I still have no idea why there were so many gentlemen with us, or even how much danger we were potentially in (or not). I have so many questions and have made up multiple scenarios in my head. But if I could do it all over again with a translator, I wouldn't. The mystery of it all was the best part of the entire experience.

KENYA

Approximately 12:30 p.m.

SAMUEL WAS VISIBLY SHIVERING by the time we reached the refuge. The last kilometre took a terrible toll, leaving him with a serious limp. I wasn't sure if it was simply cold, numb feet or if he'd been injured. Of course, he didn't complain once, and instead thanked me for staying positive and checked in on how I was feeling.

When we entered the refuge, the number of people that were inside startled me. With the severe weather I just assumed it would be empty. Instead, there were 12 British military members sitting around one long picnic table playing cards. They all looked up in our direction with equal surprise to discover they had company. When they realized we had arrived back from the other side of Mount Kenya, they were even more shocked. Their crew had been tracking the weather system for the past three days and felt it was too unsafe to proceed with their mountain training until conditions improved. The guys asked Samuel if the weather was as bad as they thought it was. He looked over at me before he responded, hesitating to say what he needed to say: "It was bad." He added, "The worst I have seen in 20 years." Then he looked over at me again with apologetic eyes. "It is not safe to go today. We could have died," he said as his voice trailed off at the end. I had divided emotions about his response. Part of me felt validated for feeling as scared as I did when we were up there, part of me was upset we went up in the first place and part of me was simply relieved we had made it.

Two of the military men grabbed my wet backpack and cleared off a bunk bed for me to sleep on for the night. It was not the first time I'd be sharing a room with multiple men (that didn't come out right), but that didn't mean it was super comfortable. I rolled my sleeping bag out on the damp foam mattress and slithered inside to warm up and read my book for a while. I needed a little time to decompress and forget about what we had been through earlier in the day. Samuel gently knocked on the room door and poked his head in after I said hello. "It will be colder soon. More rain is coming. Please use my sweater," he kindly offered as he pulled it off his shoulders. "Samuel, thank you. But I don't want you to be cold," I responded back. "Me? I am okay. Thank you," he assured me with a kind smile. I didn't believe him, but I also didn't want to offend him. I slipped his red sweater over my head and proudly wore it all night, as he wished. "Is it okay if you tell one more story before we eat?" he asked with anticipation as he sat down on the bunk across from me. "If you like," I said humbly.

CAMEROON

AS BRITNEY SPEARS SINGS, "Oops!...I did it again." That familiar nervous churn in my stomach began as I walked toward the Douala International Airport from the airplane. I'd landed in Africa without a single plan in place, feeling commitment-free and loving it. But I was also scared, knowing it had been nearly 12 months since my last adventure, which led me to worry that my travel senses were rusty. I needed to find my feet and interact with someone to get the lay of the land, quickly.

Conveniently, a Scotsman standing ahead of me at customs engaged in conversation. At five feet seven inches tall myself, I towered over the gentleman. What he lacked in height he made up for with the gift of gab and tremendous passion. I sensed right away his motivation for interacting was mostly to hear his own amazing ideas, or to get the scoop on why I was in line alone. Either way, I needed the conversation for a little distraction from my nerves and he wasn't short on things to talk about. He disclosed that his trip to Cameroon was one of several over the past decade, all for business. I was disappointed when he told stories (albeit comical and highly entertaining) that had zero positivity to them. Everything he shared involved either being stolen from or lied to or was a complaint about the food or heat. I listened patiently to be polite, and intended to use his precautions as reminders to be aware of my surroundings, but I wasn't about to let his mishaps and perceptions taint my experience. Ironically, his misadventures made me feel less nervous and more prepared because his attitude went against everything I believed.

When it was my turn to talk, I could see the gentleman was visibly confused as I explained my very loose plans to catch a taxi from the airport, drive to the village of Buea in the middle of the night and hire a random stranger from the area to guide me up Mount Cameroon. He pulled his hands out of his jeans pockets and crossed his arms across his chest, attempting to contain his nervous dithering. When I finished explaining, he continued to look up at me with squinted eyes for a few seconds, head tilted to one side, his ball cap slightly askew. We had our first awkward pause in conversation and I wasn't sure if it was because he was waiting for me to provide more information, or to announce I was joking.

When I didn't add anything further, the little detail he was given began to resonate and he became visibly disturbed. "Wait. What? You're not going with a tour company?" he asked with genuine terror in his voice. He grabbed the brim of his hat and shifted it back and forth over his forehead while he processed things further. I continued to stay quiet; it was kind of fun to see him squirm. He looked down at the floor as he collected his thoughts, then looked back up and began interrogating me. I knew it was out of concern, but I found it irritating that he was projecting his own perceptions onto me. "Where will you sleep tonight?" I naively told him that I'd find a hostel or hotel upon arrival and then begin hiking the following day with someone from the area. "So you're going to hike with a complete stranger then?" he asked with worry. "Yes, that's the plan. I don't know anyone from Cameroon, so I'll be relying on someone that knows the area well," I responded back. "Does your family know you are doing this?" he added. "Yes, they do. They aren't happy about it, but they know how much I love to travel." His response:

"Do you have self-protection, like pepper spray?" "What? No." I answered, surprised by the question. "What are you thinking?" he asked rhetorically. We had our second awkward pause as he became speechless, needing more time to let things register. I could tell he was frustrated (borderline angry) and wanted to ask more questions. Impressively, he held back in order to avoid further frustration with my lack of Cameroon knowledge and weak game plan. "It will all work out, as it should." I broke the silence with a little defensiveness in my voice, as my confidence took a hit. The intensity of his questioning made me feel naive and added a hint of doubt that I wanted to ignore. It was a red flag for my ego that I was letting a stranger's opinion impact how I was feeling about my choices. *I'm a strong, independent gal, dammit! There's no place for wishy-washiness during travel! Pull yourself together lady!*

"*C'est à qui*?" (Who's next?) the customs officer yelled out. It was a relief to have our conversation interrupted so I didn't feel like I had to explain myself further.

The energetic Scotsmen darted out of the queue and approached the counter. It was shocking how his persona morphed in the time it took to walk all of five steps forward. His relaxed posture tightened – including his smile – and his friendliness transformed into a very off-putting arrogance. No pleasantries were shared as he immediately started berating the two men behind the desk about how slow the service was. I tried to ignore their interaction, hoping they wouldn't assume we were associated, since we were the only foreigners in line. The Scotsman flailed his hands in rage while his neck turned an unflattering shade of red. I couldn't make out what the customs officers were responding back with, but the looks on their faces made it obvious this was not the highlight of their day. After a longer time than it should have taken, the Scotsman was given his passport back and he evacuated the counter space. Just as he was walking away, he unsubtly warned me of "how corrupt these guys are" and how "you can't trust anyone." If that wasn't enough, he decided it was a good idea to make a loud cringe-worthy comment about one of the gentlemen's weight. *Dude! Why did you have to say that? Come on!* I wanted to crawl into a hole. I knew he had screwed me. Even though it might not have even been his intent, I was going to pay for his outburst!

"*C'est à qui?*" the officer yelled out again. I looked up to dis-cover dark eyes filled with disdain, staring at me. *Oh yeah, I'm screwed.* The path between us seemed too close for comfort, which didn't give me very much time to sort out my thoughts. All I could come up with was "...". Yeah, absolutely nothing. I wasn't doing myself any favours. The officer swiped my passport from my hand and flipped through the pages with a very serious face for a rather long period of time. I tried to make small talk about having never been to Scotland before (subtle, I know) as he grimaced at my documents, but it was obvious I wasn't making any buddies.

After what felt like an eternity, he looked back up and requested to look inside my carry-on baggage. This was uncon-ventional and reinforced my suspicion I would be punished for the absurd Scottish lashing they had received 15 minutes prior. I cooperatively handed over my bag and attempted to look as unfazed as possible. Next, I opened my bag nice and wide to make the process simple and drama-free. *I'm being downright lovely right now. These guys will see that I'm one of the good ones.* Meanwhile, the second customs officer stepped over to participate in the fun. Together they pulled all the contents out: hiking snacks, two water bottles, a pair of clean underwear, toothbrush with paste, ChapStick, sunscreen, sunglasses, a book and a headlamp. The essentials were in my carry-on so I could hike Mount Cameroon even if my large backpack didn't make my multiple flight con-nections. The two gentlemen held up my vacuum-sealed (clearly purchased in the airport) snacks and refused to let me repack them. I clued in quickly that my sunglasses were also no longer mine when one of the guys put them on and never took them off after his buddy gave him a thumbs up in approval. My fluff romance novel and headlamp also became their keepsakes. They graciously gave everything else I owned back after manhandling it all – including my underwear. *They're just underwear, dude. I don't think it's necessary to show them to everyone in the room.* I wasn't impressed, but I wasn't going to fight about it and allow the experience to ruin my first day. I was certain more food and even sunglasses could be purchased somewhere. I repacked my remaining belongings and headed toward the baggage claim area, which sounded chaotic in the distance.

Unfortunately, standing at the entrance to the baggage claim frenzy was the Scotsman, waiting for me! He attempted to catch my attention, but I pretended I didn't see him. I felt like a jerk, but I needed a moment to shed the customs stress off. My experience there might not have been entirely his fault, but I was certain he hadn't enhanced it. I didn't owe him anything and I wasn't going to risk further trouble just to be nice. At home, I would have done the opposite, but here, alone, no way! This was the time to look after myself and what was best for me.

Nearly 30 minutes passed as I awkwardly tried to avoid eye contact with the Scotsman while waiting at the opposite end of the baggage carousel. When my bag appeared from under the rubber flaps my heart fluttered with relief and excitement. It wasn't the possession itself; it was the familiarity – a token from home that provided comfort. I lifted if off the belt and swung it over my shoulders. Its weight grounded me and reminded me of why I had flown thousands of kilometres to be standing on West African soil. I was here to do what I loved most – use my body, push it, challenge my comfort level and open my heart to as many new people and experiences as possible. I anticipated that there would be more trouble, more nerves, more discomfort, but I was ready for it.

Speaking of trouble, just as I was walking out the airport doors the Scotsman reappeared in haste. He was an annoyance I couldn't shake, but instead of getting frustrated I took the opportunity to use him for instinct practice. I needed to figure out if he was negative about Cameroon because of his experiences or had negative experiences because of an initial negative attitude. I let that question simmer in the background while I listened to his soliloquy about his baggage "clearly" being tampered with. "Obviously," someone was out to steal from him. My gut was telling me he was a harmless, emotional guy that likely got wound up about many things, even if they didn't concern him. I imagined he felt it was his duty to assist me in order to alleviate his conscience.

Without taking a breath, he finished his rant and insisted on arranging a taxi for me. He leapt from one topic to the next so quickly I didn't have a chance to refuse his offer. In seconds he was already immersed in negotiations with a driver. I didn't hear the entire conversation, but the words "respect" and "bullshit" and phrases "ever touch her" and "fuck you up" were noted. Apparently, I had myself a Scottish fixer! When the threats ended, the Scotsman spotted the driver some cash, patted me on the shoulder a couple of times and gave me his card in case of emergency. Instinct test: complete. My gut was spot on (harmless, very emotional) and it gave me so much more confidence. I was ready to experience Cameroon! "You're a crazy lassie! I can't believe you're doing this. I'm going to leave you with some final advice. Listen to me! Don't go out at night – that would be strike one. Don't trust anyone – that's a definite strike two. Don't drink or eat anything weird – that would be strike three. And don't smile so much for fuck sakes! If you don't follow the rules, then you'll be out!" These were his final motivational words to me. I looked down at his card to catch his name: Fergus. I shook his hand and hollered back at him as I stepped into the front seat of the taxi, "Fergus, what kind of baseball do you play in Scotland? Four strikes and I'm out? And how am I supposed to have any fun with these restrictions?" I gave him a cheeky grin, just to give him a hard time. He smiled back, shook his head and threw his hands up in the air like he had given up all hope for me. "Stop smiling, dammit!" he yelled back at the last minute.

The drive to Buea, a town bordering the eastern slopes of Mount Cameroon, was about two hours from the airport. It was nearly dark by the time we left, so my initial view of Cameroon was limited to periodic silhouettes of locals walking and biking on the sides of the highway. We arrived late in the evening with the priority to find a place where I could rest my eyes after a full day and a half of travel. My only criteria on a place to stay: cheap. The taxi driver, named Ahmed, stopped at one location that he recommended, unfortunately discovering it had no vacancy. His second choice was also at full capacity. An hour later, and every option exhausted, I was left with no accommodation. The last hotel manager informed us that the president of Cameroon was arriving in Buea any day and all of the sleeping establishments were occupied by out-of-town diplomats in anticipation of his arrival. In addition to this sleeping inconvenience, he informed us that all food markets, stores and banks would be closed for the next few days in celebration. Some restaurants would open but would only be accommodating the out-of-town representatives.

This unsettling information was misaligned with my every-thing-works-out attitude. I had no place to sleep and no way of purchasing food to replace the items that were taken earlier. Oddly, the first person that came to mind was Fergus; he would be mortified if he knew what I had gotten myself into already. I could just hear him: " You should have booked something online before you left Canada, to secure a bed." Then there was an echo:

"You should book online before you visit Buea." Ahmed was apparently channelling Fergus and continuing his lecture! I knew how this looked. (Yeah, you can say it out loud to yourself, but I won't be able to hear you.) A huge part of the travel experience for me is the spontaneity and finding adventure in the unknown. Life at home is rigid: organized with deadlines, appointments and every other minute accounted for. It's refreshing to let all plans and control go and see what unfolds. It feels so free! Unfortunately, homelessness and starvation are apparent risks that can come along with this relaxed approach. Just an FYI.

So I had a situation on my hands. Strike one: don't go out at night. *Oops.* I felt terrible asking Ahmed to continue driving me from one place to the next at such an hour, so around midnight I planned to set my hiking tent up outside of town. I'd figure my basic necessities out in the morning, after some sleep. Ahmed was a lovely, patient man and kindly discouraged my plans without telling me I was a complete moron. "I think it is very good to have you at the taxi station tonight. It is very close and no one will be there. It will be comfortable for you," he promised. It was a generous offer and one that I accepted with gratitude.

The air was warm and the sky was speckled with stars as I stepped out of the car and walked toward a small dark-coloured building with a corrugated metal roof. There were no signs indicating this was a taxi station. It certainly was a red flag, but I also couldn't be certain that I just misunderstood what he was suggesting earlier. Maybe he said *next* to the taxi office? I was so tired I wasn't thinking clearly. I walked blindly into the building after Ahmed as he fiddled around to find a light.

He turned a lantern on and exposed an open room that looked similar to what an office lounge at home would look like. A painted yellow concrete floor with a table and three mismatched chairs were in the centre of the room. A few posters of the community of Buea, a map of Cameroon and a photo of the president himself were on the wall. A small kitchen area was off to our right side and two bedrooms were in the back for staff members. I couldn't quite tell if it was an office or a home or both. Regardless, it was obvious I wasn't in any danger and Ahmed was paying me a huge favour. I felt guilty for questioning him even for a moment. Ahmed offered one of the available beds, but I opted to take a place on the floor instead. It would have felt strange to sleep in someone else's bed. Sleeping on the floor of a taxi station, on the other hand, totally normal, obviously. He helped me lay my sleeping bag down and set the lantern beside me in case I needed a light to navigate my way to the toilet outside. *Hmm. A headlamp would be handy right about now. Damn those guys! Okay, time to move on now sister.* I kept all of my clothes on, 100 per cent out of paranoia that someone would walk in on a middle-aged white girl. (Nobody needed to see that.) I wiggled into my sleeping bag and fell asleep within minutes.

I don't remember the remainder of the evening, but I was woken up by a beautiful ray of sun jutting out from under one of the ridges of the corrugated metal roof. Ahmed walked in through the door with a big smile, holding two loaves of unsliced bread, two bottles of water and a jar of mayonnaise to take on my hike. A nostalgic memory of my dad coming home early with Egg McMuffins when we were kids came over me in that exact moment. I was touched by his thought and effort, just as I was many years ago with my dad; it made me feel safe. I unzipped myself from the sleeping bag and sipped on some bottled water while I took in my surroundings. In the daylight I decided that the building was definitely a business, not a home. But it had been home to me the past few hours, and I was so thankful for Ahmed's kindness and hospitality.

Ahmed explained to me that he had asked his nephew and his friend to guide me up and down Mount Cameroon. They would arrive at the taxi station in a few hours, after they packed and walked over. Naturally, it was the perfect opportunity to tuck in a short workout to get the body primed and ready for the day! Ahmed laughed and shook his head at my pre-hiking plans. But then he disclosed that he too was an avid fitness enthusiast. "Well then, what do you have going on for the next hour or so?" I asked him. "Not much. Waiting for the boys to come, so you can meet," he responded casually. "Want to work out with me quickly before they arrive?" I asked in hopes he'd agree and satisfy my curiosity about what his fitness routine entailed. "I think I will say yes. Okay," he responded with a smile and a shake of his head in disbelief at my unexpected request. (I could tell he was just as curious!)

He removed his jacket, rolled up his shirtsleeves and got down on the floor and started pumping out push-ups like a beast. *Well hot damn, Ahmed's got some pipes!* I joined in and asked how many we were going to do. "As many as you can, until you cannot," he spoke between grunts. "Shit, what?" I panted back with a little joyous giggle. Ahmed did about 100 push-ups (no joke) and I have no idea how many I did. That's a total lie. I just don't want to look pathetic in comparison. It was my turn to select the next exercise. I chose back lunges and demonstrated while Ahmed cocked his head to the side with confusion. "Ah yes! Step backs," he responded. That was a new term for me, but it was perhaps a better descriptor than lunges anyway. He grabbed a chair and handed it to me. I interpreted this as putting one foot on top to perform a single leg lunge. I was wrong. He held his chair up over his head and began his step backs. "You try!" he directed with incredible enthusiasm. He was so nice, and so excited, I couldn't say no. I held the chair above my head like he was, noticing right away I wasn't dealing with a plastic IKEA product. After I completed ten repetitions on each side with Ahmed's approval of my technique, he joined in and started the countdown. "We have 50 more. Fifty, 49, 48...You can do it!" This was karma. He was speaking *my* personal training language and there was no way I could quit. Just like my clients, I didn't want to let him down.

It was Ahmed's turn to choose the third exercise and I was scared about what he'd come up with. *This guy is a machine!* His choice was more push-ups and I vetoed it because he just wanted to show off. He grinned his toothless smile and winked at me as he scratched his salt and pepper hair to buy time to think of a good response. To my delight, he shamelessly owned it. "Yes. I am good at them! Let me just show you one more time how good." We both laughed simultaneously at his cheekiness, and then dropped to the floor for one more push-up extravaganza. "Okay, you win Ahmed. I can't do any more push-ups. Next exercise." I gave in after way more than I thought I had in me. Ahmed's pace had drastically slowed down, but he was still going.

Time flew by as we continued back and forth with exercise challenges and harmless banter. It wasn't until we heard footsteps outside the front door that we realized what time it was. Two teens, introduced as Lucien and Joseph, strolled through just as we were getting creative with our workout. The look on their faces was priceless. Lucien, tall and slender, stood in shock with a wide-open, gigantic smile. Joseph, short and stalky, squinted his eyes like he was looking at the sun. Ahmed and I were found pressed back-to-back, supporting each other on the way up and down as we executed simultaneous squats. We were both sweating profusely and grunting in blissful exercise discomfort.

"Boys! This is Anyela," Ahmed introduced me with an enthusiastic accent. We awkwardly peeled our backs off each other and greeted the guys. Ahmed wiped the sweat from his forehead and instantly transformed into the professional planner.

"These two boys can be trusted. They are strong and can guide you on Mount Cameroon," Ahmed promised with a confident smile. I had no plans in place and the opportunity to hike with two locals was an ideal scenario in my mind. *Everything always works out, just like I said it would to Fergus.* I really felt Ahmed had my best interests at heart. If he thought these two would be trustworthy guides, I was all in. *This is going to be awesome! Two young fit dudes. We are going to fly up that mountain!* We negotiated a fee for their service and briefly talked about the hike. "The walk is easy. Then steepy, steepy. Then less steepy. Then steepy. Then slowly, slowly down and not too steepy," Lucien described. "There are three camps. If you are strong..." Joseph began to explain. "She is very strong," Ahmed interjected with confidence. "Then we will pass camp one and sleep our first night at camp two today. It is already late, so we must walk quickly to make it before dark," Joseph finished. I was flattered that Ahmed thought I was strong, but now I had pressure to perform. Nerves began to build and I was immediately regretting those box jumps we did onto Ahmed's desk earlier. *Whose dumb idea had that been anyway? Oh right, mine.*

There was almost no preparation needed for the journey. We had all the food we could get our hands on, and with the exception of me having to stuff my sleeping bag into my bag, we were all packed. I shook Ahmed's hand with gratitude and the three of us set off. Ahmed stood at the doorway of the building and hollered out to the boys as we walked to the street to catch a ride: "Take very good care of her. Good luck." I found it ironic that we were hitchhiking from a taxi station, but I decided that I'd just go along with it.

The day started with a short 12-km drive to the base of Mount Cameroon. Many of the streets were closed off in anticipation of accommodating the president and his entourage. It was early enough in the day that we were able to make our commute fairly easily without any traffic. When we were dropped off, we pulled our bags on our backs and set off into the forest. The trail was a single track and mild in elevation. We walked single file, passing farmland and small villages crowded with several children waving and smiling, hoping to have their photos taken. We took our time and enjoyed their company as they ran toward us and used every opportunity to touch my pale skin and inspect things I wouldn't have imagined to be interesting. My teeth and fingernails were strangely mesmerizing! Birds were chirping and the boys pointed out insects and plants that were of interest. I had read that black mamba snakes were sometimes seen in the Mount Cameroon region. I asked the guys if they had ever seen one, mostly out of curiosity, not out of too much concern, anticipating it would likely be a rare sighting. If it weren't for the simultaneous "no" I received, I wouldn't have questioned their answer. "Really, never? Well, if not black mambas, what about other snakes?" I asked, hoping they'd either convince me that it was indeed never, or come out with an apology and explain that they had seen snakes a few times, but it was uncommon and they didn't want to worry me. Instead, all I got was a diversion. "This plant is very beautiful," Lucien pointed out. The non-answer was my answer.

From that point on, I was just a bit more careful where I placed my foot when I stepped forward. We approached camp one and were welcomed by several park rangers. They were playing cards and listening to Nigerian gospel music in the shade. The vibe was relaxed and fun. We stayed long enough for all of us to use the outhouse and drink a few rationed sips of water. I was receiving mixed messages all afternoon. One minute I was told to walk quickly to beat the dark, the next minute I was told to not worry and slow down. I just went along with it and attempted to understand whether there was any reasoning behind it. I figured there wasn't and it was just two inexperienced "guides" trying to look like they knew what they were doing. I found it entertaining and kind of endearing. They clearly knew where to go, but I didn't get the impression they really knew what they were doing or had a lot of mountain hiking experience. Strike two: don't trust anyone. *Oops.*

The trail became much steeper and transitioned from dirt to rock as we left the rainforest behind us. The higher we went, the smaller the rocks became. The hiking was spectacular! As a fitness trainer, by spectacular I mean the climb between camp one and two was approximately 300 vertical metres. My calves were burning, and my lungs were being tested. It felt SO good! As we trekked up, the clouds rolled in and hid the territory we had already covered. With blue sky above and a sheet of thick grey cloud below, it felt like we were in heaven. The food situation was the only reminder that we were not. Between the three of us it was certainly not a lot of fuel for the number of kilometres we were walking, especially when reaching a summit altitude at 4095 m. It was late afternoon and not one of us had eaten anything on the trail. I was amazed at our pace, considering how hungry and tired we all were. I was especially surprised after Ahmed had tried to annihilate my legs during our workout. *I think he was trying to kill me this morning. More like my ego was!*

When we marched our way into camp two, we discovered that someone had set fire (intentionally or unintentionally) to the refuge, and it had completely burnt down. The boys were devastated and confused as to how something like this could have happened. The soil was black and there was little protection from the elements, so the decision to push to camp three was an easy one. The trail continued to be fairly steep and likely felt more strenuous because of our hunger. We arrived at camp three exhausted and oddly satisfied with the speed we had maintained up the mountain. We pulled out the bread and mayonnaise and carefully divided up our portions. It might have been the best bread I've ever eaten.

We set up our tents and nestled in almost immediately. I once again did not remember the night. I slept until the sun pleasantly lit up my tent in the early morning.

We decided as a group to save the remaining bread for later in the day and skipped breakfast. We packed up our tents and left for the summit. The sun continued to shine and all evidence of cloud from the previous day was gone. My backpack felt tender on my hips and its weight felt much heavier. Evidently, I wasn't alone because Joseph described how he was feeling at every possible opportunity. "My body feels like a rhino ran over it. It is angry." There would be a pause for a few minutes and then he'd interject with a little more detail. "Ooh, it is aaaaangryy! Like an elephant went walking, walking, walking over and over this part here [he pressed on the front of his legs]. Ooh, and here [he pressed on the back of both calves]." I just laughed and happily anticipated the next hilarious chapter of his saga. It wasn't what you'd expect from your hiking "guide" – especially from one nearly ten years younger. Lucien reacted to his narrative from time to time with his gift of repartee. "I feel very fine. Joseph, you are like an old person. Anyela can carry you like a very small baby, if you like." The minute Lucien squirmed under the weight of his bag and took a pause to catch his breath, Joseph retaliated with a reminder of who was oldest. "Old man, try to keep up!" he bugged with an innocent smirk.

The last push to the top was much more gradual and felt very easy compared to what we'd walked the previous day. It was entertaining just how much the boys were suffering and complaining, especially on the easy day. The sun continued to radiate down, but the wind whipped around us, providing a reminder of how high our elevation was. Our steps became slower and our breath more laboured as a result of the thinner air, but the exhilarating feeling in making the final approach overshadowed it.

We had made it – 4095 m. We had a three-way hug with the sign between our feet. Lucien and Joseph were hooting and hollering and laughing with joy. We sat down on the rocks to take in the glorious view and embraced the sun on our faces. You could see for miles, thanks to the clear blue sky. Joseph explained to me that the Indigenous name for Mount Cameroon was Mongo ma Ndemi, meaning mountain of greatness. Lucien said it was the highest point in sub-Saharan western and central Africa and ranked number four in elevation for all of Africa. They spoke with such pride in their home country, and it made it that much more special to experience it with them. Like I always do, I made a point to appreciate my two feet planted on the summit and captured a picture. *I will likely never stand on this mountain again in my lifetime. Take it all in.* I observed every sense independently in the hopes that I could one day, years later, close my eyes and slip right back into that blissful moment in time. I soaked in the view of the horizon kilometres down below, the smiles of satisfaction on the guys' faces, the powerful gusts of air that nudged me side to side, the tingling in my fingertips from the cold, the taste of blood from my cracked lips, the burn from the sun on my eyelids, the lightness in my body sans backpack, the throbbing pressure points on the balls of my feet, the howls and whistles of the wind that blocked out all other sound, and the extra work I felt my heart making to accommodate the effort required to exist at that elevation.

I took one final look at the view and one deep breath of the pure air. It was so clean it smelled like I was the first to ever use it. Then I turned to the boys in agreement – it was time to walk down.

We made our descent slow and steady off Mount Cameroon's highest point, Fako peak. The trail made large switchbacks through fine scree, making it an enjoyable transition down.

After a few hours, we found ourselves walking on large volcanic rocks with various sized volcanoes surrounding us. I'd never seen so many volcanoes in one area. It felt like we were on another planet! My head was on a swivel as I navigated over the rock beneath me and tried to take in the mystifying view. There wasn't a single other person or hint of habitation anywhere. The ability to see places that are only accessible by foot is something I'm extremely grateful for. The rock rubble surrounding us was black and most of the trees and grass matched since they had been completely burnt. It was obvious we were walking on dried lava from a previous eruption not long ago.

An eerie fog slithered in and glazed over the earth at hip height. It built in thickness and shifted over time, creating a wall of mystery obstructing our view of what lay ahead. We kept our pace and walked directly into it, discovering it was thicker than we thought. For about an hour all I could see was white, making it difficult to track Lucien and Joseph in front of me. To help us stay together, Joseph sang some of his favourite songs so we could follow his voice. There was creepiness to our surroundings, but it also provided an unexpected feeling of calm due to the lack of visual distraction. I focused on Joseph's incredible singing voice carrying through the natural amphitheatre, the caress of the fog on my cheeks and the clean air I took in with intention. My body was tired, I was hungry, I had no clue where I was and I couldn't have been happier.

The fog eventually disintegrated with the help of the sun, and a beautiful golden field was exposed. The trail undulated gently for hours as I grazed my hands over the tips of the grass as we cut through. Our elevation declined and the temperature increased. I took my coat off while we sat in the meadow and shared the last of our bread. With the humidity and the plastic bag it was wrapped in, our bread had grown an impressive amount of mould (also known as African spice, according to Lucien and Joseph). We picked the bluish green pieces off and ate the white parts. It was amazing how yesterday it had been the best bread I'd eaten in my life and today it was the worst.

We slung our bags back on and moved our way out of the grassland. We entered the edge of the forest and set up our camp.

We were officially out of food and very hungry. At times it was slightly painful in the belly, then it would subside and I felt like I could go for hours without more sustenance. The three of us scattered and looked for twigs and sticks to start a fire. When I returned to our camp, there was nobody there. I could see Lucien and Joseph standing with a very tall man in the distance. *Where did he come from? Am I hallucinating?* I walked in their direction to confirm I wasn't losing it. *He's real! At least I'm not going crazy.* The stranger saw me coming and turned away immediately. The boys walked toward me in haste and escorted me away from where they were originally standing.

As we scurried toward our campsite, they leaned in and whispered, "That is the Bush Man! He is a local hunter that visits the lower camps sometimes. It is our first time seeing him, but we hear stories." "What stories?" I asked with concern. "Is he dangerous?" Lucien answered, "No, not dangerous. He hunts and doesn't speak very much." Joseph gave Lucien a look that was unsettling and led me to ask, "Hey! What was that look? Do you know something and are not wanting to scare me?" "No. He does not smile or laugh or speak. He frightens people because they do not understand him. He is..."

Joseph paused as soon as we heard the quiet footsteps behind us. When we turned around, there stood the Bush Man. If I had to guess, he was about six foot six, even without shoes. He wore an oversized cotton dress shirt that hung over his lean frame. One of the arms was torn at the shoulder seam and half the buttons were missing, so the shirt was misaligned to keep it closed. I couldn't make out the details of his face in the dark, but he was intensely gazing at the boys with no obvious facial expression. I instantly felt nervous, despite not being a part of his focus. The boys tensed up and couldn't hide their uneasiness. Without saying anything, he raised his long arm and Joseph flinched in fear. He promptly felt embarrassed when he realized the Bush

Man was merely pointing to an area of our camp where he was requesting to sleep. Lucien took charge and nodded in agreement that he could sleep in our little camp clearing. The Bush Man slowly reached into his pocket and pulled a dead squirrel out. He handed it to Lucien and then walked over to his sleeping quarters to lie down.

The three of us sat for a moment in silence until I broke it with another question. "Did he catch that squirrel with his bare hands? I didn't see any tools or weapons." I asked partially out of curiosity and partially to assure them I wasn't too freaked out to chit-chat. "Yes, he is very fast. He moves very quickly," Lucien remarked. As Joseph assembled the fire to cook the squirrel for dinner, Lucien eased our minds about our unexpected company. "Be free. He is hunting. Do not worry. He is gentle."

The crackle of the fire was soothing. I watched its flames writhe around the meal we were generously gifted. When it was ready, Joseph pulled it apart and we shared it between the three of us. We invited the Bush Man to join us, but he seemed content to lie on the dirt a few metres away. Joseph told tales of his unorthodox hunting style, but Lucien and I didn't believe it until we saw it for ourselves that evening. The Bush Man remained on the ground and meticulously baited his body with what looked like breadcrumbs to entice the mice to scurry up out of the grass onto his legs and chest. Once they were within reach, he'd snatch them up one by one and put them inside a black garbage bag to deprive them of air. Dozens were crawling over his body at one time.

Lucien and Joseph did a much better job of not staring. I wanted to be polite, but I found myself looking over constantly with disbelief and fascination. It was incredible how fast he could snatch those rodents up! His hands were so large the mice looked like little caterpillars comparatively. At no point while watching this unfold did I even consider the copious volume of rodents surrounding us until it was time to crawl on the ground to get into my single-man tent. I looked in every cranny to be sure I didn't have company, then double-checked that I had a tight zipper closure. I could hear little squeaks around me all night long, paired with the rustle of the Bush Man's plastic bag. For self-preservation I refused to let the notion of mice nibbling on the tent be a possibility. But, just in case, I kept my sleeping bag zipped all the way up with just my face poking out, once again. This seemed to be a familiar occurrence on my vacations.

The next morning I opened my eyes and hesitantly scanned my tent for possible intruders. My trusty tent held up once more! I crawled out the front and found Joseph with a snake wrapped around a stick. "More food!" he proudly shared. "Is that a black mamba?" I asked jokingly, after our earlier conversation. In my mind there was no way it was an actual black mamba. "Yes. It is," he said with no inflection in his voice, not making eye contact. "I thought you said –" He cut me off. "My English is not too good." "Your English is just fine!" I said while laughing at his ridiculous excuse. *I knew those guys were lying! I suspected it the whole time. No sense in getting upset. I'm certain they were just trying to make me feel comfortable.* I let him off the hook and asked warily, "Are we going to eat that for breakfast?" He explained, "Yes. I will cook him on the fire."

If that wasn't enough to wake up to, I looked over at the Bush Man and he had successfully filled his entire garbage bag with vermin. *Where the hell am I right now?* I decided right then and there he was the most hardcore man I'd ever encountered. He was still lying down, eyes closed, with his one-inch (at least) thick calloused feet facing me. His toes were twice the thickness of anyone else's toes. No, I don't typically make it a point to look at other people's feet. This was just an extraordinary circumstance. I guessed by the incredible density of his skin that he could walk across shards of glass and not even get a cut. *I wonder if he has ever worn a pair of shoes in his life? I feel silly wearing these GORE-TEX hiking boots in his presence, although I haven't felt an ounce of judgment from him at any point.* In fact, I felt quite the opposite; there was a feeling of acceptance and peacefulness from him – even when smothering furry critters.

I swivelled my head back to Joseph as he prepared the snake. The process was new to me and I was greatly interested to learn and observe. But just as he was peeling the skin back I felt a gentle tap on my arm. I turned my head and was face to face with a familiar tattered, brown, button-up dress shirt. I didn't hear or see him coming, but as I raised my head I knew my eyes would meet the Bush Man's. He once again had no expression on his weathered face. The deep creases in his forehead and around his mouth indicated he might be in his 70s, but his body was lean and muscular like a 35-year-old's. It was impossible to know his age.

I was startled and surprised by how close he was standing to me. I wouldn't have expected him to be comfortable with close human distancing. It took me a moment to register why he had caught my attention. His grey eyes stared into mine as if he were trying to speak to me. Once I was fixated on him, he slowly looked down toward his leathery hand and guided my gaze to what he was offering. He had three suffocated mice. The Bush Man gently lifted my hand, which looked shockingly small and white in his, and placed the mice in my palm. They felt warm and a little prickly. He pointed to Lucien, then Joseph, then me and made an eating motion by bringing his fingers to his mouth. He was kindly offering us each a mouse for breakfast. I was between crying out of gratitude and shitting my pants with intimidation. I nodded to indicate I understood, and smiled to say thank you. He nodded back, then slowly turned and walked away with his bag of mice under one arm and the other casually swaying back and forth like he had nowhere to be anytime soon. That was the last time we saw him.

"Lucien! The Bush Man gave Anyela food!" Joseph whispered, with astonishment. "What did he say?" Lucien asked me. "He was giving me his special mouse recipe that include –" Lucian laughed, "Okay, okay, you're funny! He said no words. Good joke." I said, "Let's cook these mice up while we try the snake!" A sentence I never thought I'd ever say. Strike three: don't drink or eat anything weird. *Oops.*

The snake was quite small and the meat had no taste, but I certainly wasn't going to complain. I was grateful for what I was offered. I expected the meat to be chewy for some reason, but it was quite dry and boney. The boys didn't seem to like it very much either, but it was something. There was zero rationalization for my thought process, but I felt okay with eating a deadly snake but had reservations about trying a mouse. When Joseph handed me a little piece of meat, I graciously said no thank you, as thoughts of contracting a disease entered my mind. He insisted, out of concern for my energy level, but I assured him I'd make it.

In a very short period of time we had become very comfortable with one another. As a result, the boys extinguished the fire with their pee because we had no water, and then we left our final camp that morning. We took our time walking through the forest, passing small villages and waving to the adorable children as we strolled through. We were notified by one of the women in the village that the town of Buea would still be shut down by the time we walked off Mount Cameroon. Instantly, Joseph turned and lectured me, "See, you needed the mouse for energy." He was absolutely right. I didn't feel it at the time, but had I known how much further we'd have to walk, I likely would have made a different choice.

The vegetation around us got thicker, the trail more defined by local foot traffic, and the air became warmer. Nearing the bottom, we were all in anticipation of what state the community would be in. *Will it be chaotic or peaceful during an occasion of this magnitude?*

When we turned the final corner and stepped into a clearing that led us down to the highway, we were alone. There were very few houses with anyone in them, and no cars on the street. It was apparent almost every individual was situated in the town of Buea to get an in-person view of the president. This was a very momentous time, yet Lucien and Joseph didn't seem to have the excitement I thought they'd have. They were more interested in charging their phones to make a call for a ride back to town. They didn't want to walk anymore!

We stopped at multiple homes in an attempt to access power, but nobody was around. We continued to walk down the centre of the empty highway until we were hollered at by a group of military. We passed over to the side of the road and explained our situation. I didn't understand the conversation because it wasn't in English, but the military men kept looking at Lucien and Joseph, and then over to me, then back to them, then back to me (this time with concern), then back to them. Whatever was said allowed Lucien to borrow their power bank so he could charge his phone for a few minutes.

Our original plan was to call Ahmed when we made it back to the highway so he could drive us home. Twenty minutes passed and we finally had enough cell power to connect a call. On the phone, Ahmed explained that no cars were permitted on the roads because the president would be escorted in one to two hours through town and up to the gated residence where he would be staying. Lucien shook his head in disbelief and relayed what Ahmed told him. "We must walk. Only diplomats can drive on this very road. I think we are very strong and we can do it." I think it was as much positivity as he could muster. It was nearly 35 degrees Celsius; we had no water, near empty stomachs and no additional food. It was going to be a struggle, but I too knew we could do it. I just shook my head and laughed (internally) at the timing again. It was inconvenient enough to arrive when I had, but to be on the precise road that the president would be taking to his residence within hours of our descent? I couldn't have planned this any worse.

The three of us trudged down the paved highway toward town, looking particularly dishevelled. After about an hour I was turning into a pink zombie, thanks to the scorching sun. Joseph kept touching my forearm out of concern and awe for how red it was. "Is it stingy?" he asked. "You are very pinky-pinky. It is the same colour of the fruits we eat. It looks angry!" he added, with a hilarious and appropriate description. "It doesn't feel very nice, but I'll be okay!" I assured him.

I looked down at my hands and they had swelled from the heat to the point where I could no longer bend my fingers. I was in need of some water and it would be a long time before we got some. I didn't want the guys to notice my mobility issue and worry, so instead of awkwardly trying to untie my shirt from around my waist to use it as sun protection, I collected a plastic bag from the ditch and wrapped my hands in that instead. Hiking in Africa is super glam! It wasn't that long ago my sunglasses had been taken and I was worried about not finding cool ones to replace them. This situation was like that, but not at all. *This* was an actual problem. Life really is about perspective. The dust and debris from the bag stuck to my sweaty, moist skin. It felt like glitter had exploded all over my face and neck. It was impossible to get off, so I just left it as it was. I had given up on appearances and was focusing my attention on making it to our destination, preferably with some skin still left.

In my distracted state I didn't notice the black suburban convoy approaching us right away. About 500 metres ahead on our side of the road more military had lined up at the intersection. They held their guns close as they tracked our every move toward them. When we were within talking distance, one of the men began to interrogate us with a very aggressive whisper: "Why are you walking here? Do you have a camera? Do you know that the president is coming right now? You cannot take photos!" One of the military grabbed Joseph by the arm and pulled him to the side of the road with such aggression that he tore his T-shirt. Lucien and I immediately moved in the same direction to avoid our own manhandling. "You stay here. Do not move. Do not take photos! The president is coming!" the man demanded while pressing the side of his rifle across our chests to hold us in place.

There was an initial excitement in the air with the president's arrival, but then it quickly shifted to tension. Lucien and Joseph had palpable rage for how we were being treated, and my nerves sensed one or both of the boys were about to retaliate. I leaned in and whispered as quietly as I could to hide any indication there was an issue from the armed gatekeeper. "It's okay guys. Let's respect the orders and then we can move on." Both boys stood rigid, arms crossed with infuriated grimaces. It was obvious they didn't agree with my recommendation. "Get your gun off!" Lucien yelled over my head. The military man smirked then ignored him and continued to look down the highway for signs of the president.

I didn't like that we were being treated like we were less than, and having a gun pressed up against us was certainly offensive, but we were in no position to win a war with them. I strongly felt our best option was to cooperate and move on in peace. In my mind, we would laugh about this later and discuss what jerks they were over a beer when we got home. The boys felt differently and continued to simmer. I was surprised by the intensity of their reaction to the situation. It was only a matter of time before they said or did something regrettable, so my gut told me to intervene. I'd made the mistake of getting screwed by someone else's rage earlier in the trip; I wasn't about to make the same mistake twice.

My mind raced with options to help defuse the situation and maintain peace. *Do I cry and make a scene? Do I speak to the military and ask for a little more consideration? Do I crack a joke to try and ease tension? Do I pretend I'm sick and try to divert things?* I was involved by association, so I had to step in before Lucien or Joseph had an outburst. In seconds I decided my best option was to threaten the boys and give them no choice but to side with me in cooperating, even if they didn't agree. With only one chance I had to play dirty and get my point across sternly and abruptly, with no pushback. I decided to use Ahmed against them, because I knew they respected him and wouldn't want to ever let him down. As I prepared to threaten them, my entire body tightened as I leaned in toward Lucien and Joseph and whispered through gritted teeth and widened eyes: "For YOUR safety and MINE, do NOT say a word, do NOT move. If something happens to YOU or ME, Ahmed will never forgive you. Do NOT get US shot. DO YOU understand?" I glared at them with an intensity I'm not sure I've ever had in my life until that moment. Lucien's eyes seemed incapable of blinking, like he was seeing a ghost. He slowly whispered, "Okay." I scared Joseph so much he couldn't even speak. He just nodded in agreement with equally wide eyes. "Thank you," I replied back as calmly as I could.

My heart continued to pound out of discomfort and fear. I wanted to believe the boys, but I kept my guard up, just in case. We stood together shoulder to shoulder in silence and waited like puppets. I could feel Joseph's escalated breathing through the rapid rise and fall of his arm next to mine. The boys' tension was still there, but it had shifted from rage toward the military to utter shock from what the heck just happened to smiley Anyela. I wasn't sure either, and I felt terrible, but I had to be okay with it. If I scared them enough to prevent a fight, I'd done what I needed to.

Minutes later, a huge line of immaculate black Suburban vehicles approached us as a surveillance helicopter flew overhead simultaneously. It was estimated that there were over

500 diplomats and a comparable number of vehicles in town to serve and protect the president. It was no wonder I wasn't able to find a place to stay! As the vehicles slowly turned one by one in through the gates across the street from us, the military guard smacked his rifle against us as a warning not to move. *Wow, that was a little unnecessary, don't yah think? It must be crummy to live so angrily. I think he needs a puppy or a workout routine!* It was unnecessary to have the gun across us in the first place, let alone smacking us with it. It was clear to me we were being used as props to enhance his tough-guy look for when the president passed. It was infuriating, but it wasn't worth a battle we'd never win. Lucien turned his head and scowled at him. I jumped in right away, "DON'T do a thing. DON'T." I didn't blame them for how they were feeling. I too wanted to kick some ass, but it would end very poorly – mostly because I was 100 per cent sure none of us had the muscle or skill required. My body tensed then slowly released when the boys stood still and looked forward, fighting the urge to say something. That proved the strength Lucien and Joseph had, how much they respected Ahmed and that I'd made the right choice.

Seconds later a very welcome distraction arrived: President Biya himself. He lowered his tinted window to greet us as his driver slowly rolled the SUV past at the slowest of paces. Everything else blurred in the background when the president looked directly into my eyes and smiled. *Ha! He totally looked right at me!* It reminded me of similar interactions I'd had at concerts with lead singers. He then waved and gave thanks for visiting his beautiful country. I didn't want to jump to conclusions, but I was pretty sure he was talking to me. After all, I was the only "pinky-pinky" person with silly hardcore boots and a backpack on. Let's just say, I wasn't blending in as much as I wanted to, especially when I realized I still had a plastic bag on when I awkwardly lifted my conjoined hands in an effort to wave back.

Lucien and Joseph waved politely but didn't seem as fasci-
nated as I was. They were more intrigued with the rims on the
vehicles and the cleanliness of the polished paint. Seeing the
president just a few feet away was surreal, but the entourage of
vehicles that led him was indeed almost as interesting. His Suburban turned the right corner into the gated area in front of us
and was followed by at least 50 more, perfectly distanced apart.
The precision and organization of the assembly was contradictory to the more typical randomness and uncertainty I loved
about Africa. Seeing the stark contrast highlighted this for me
and mesmerized the boys. When the final Suburban passed, I
felt the release of the gun from my chest. The experience had
been captivating enough for me to forget it was still on us. "You
can go," the military man announced. *That's it? All of that stress
and macho aggression and all you can say is, "You can go"?* I had so
many questions but chose to ask nothing. Just in case, I bugged
my eyes out with threat toward the boys as a reminder not to say
anything to cause unnecessary trouble. Joseph got the message
loud and clear and mouthed, "Okay!" while Lucien just started to
walk, no questions asked.

We didn't have a lot of privacy on the road like earlier on. There
were military troops in small groups everywhere. We walked in
silence and kept ourselves entertained by kicking a single stone
all the way to town. We alternated kicks between the three of us
and heckled anyone (Lucien, mostly) who kicked it off the pavement. When we ran out of road, Joseph picked the rock up and
tucked it into my backpack. "A piece of Cameroon," he said with
a grin. "A memory of Lucien and his very bad football!"

There were thousands of people in the streets of Buea upon
our arrival late in the afternoon. Women were dressed in beautiful gowns and men in handsome suits. Many of the locals
were also wearing fabric with the president's face printed on it.
Cameroon flags were waving and signs had been fixed to houses,

trees and fences celebrating his first visit to Buea in 15 years. If the three of us had not been so exhausted, we likely would have joined the party. Instead, we wearily walked through the crowd toward our starting destination. It felt like months, not days, since we'd departed.

When I laid eyes on the taxi station it came as a surprise just how much it felt like arriving home. I'd only stayed one night, but it was a comfort to be somewhere familiar, especially when Ahmed stepped outside to greet us. His warm, bright smile radiated toward us. Lucien and Joseph simultaneously dove in for a group hug as they cheered in celebration and relief. Ahmed walked over and joined in.

We sat against the outside of the taxi station and passed a bottle of water between us. Ahmed sliced off sections of mango while we reminisced about our trek. "The face Anyela had!" Lucien said, referring back to my defusion tactic. With no restored mobility yet, I took the bottle of water from Joseph using the heels of my hands and raised it to my lips. "I was worried you were going to start a fight!" I finally explained. "Yes. I was. I wanted to fight that man very much. He deserved it," Lucien confirmed. "So Anyela saved you from getting your ass whooped!" Ahmed established with zero doubt in his voice. "We must have a beer to celebrate this. I will get a big one," Ahmed announced while he stood up and imagined the scenario, laughing at the absurdity of it all. Lucien and Joseph grinned at each other in agreement. They too knew they had no chance!

Beer in one hand and wet towel in the other, Ahmed passed the lager around and gently wrapped my hands in the fabric. It felt so good to have them covered in something a little cool. He then tossed water over Lucien and Joseph as they both sat with their heads between their knees to relieve their dizziness. Ahmed sat next to me on the ground and kindly placed a slice of mango in my mouth since my hands were unusable. "So you came all the way from Canada...for all this?" Ahmed asked with a chuckle and a shake of his head. He knew that I loved every bit of it. "This is nothing, you should see what we do in Canada for fun!" I winked at him, as I nudged him with my shoulder.

I was generously offered another night at the taxi station, but I was in need of a good meal and a bed. It was no easy task, but Ahmed was able to coordinate a ride for me back to the capital city. The streets of Buea were still closed, so my only option was to walk to the edge of town to meet the gentleman who would drive me. I held back tears as I hugged Lucien, Joseph and Ahmed goodbye. In a very short period of time we had been through a lot together. We'd shared our thoughts, opinions and stories for hours while we navigated the beautiful Cameroon landscape. This was not a typical hiking experience for any of us. I believe it's a part of why we connected like we did. Joseph gave me a pat on the shoulder and handed me a folded note. "It is the song you liked at camp one with the park rangers. To remind you of your African home," he said quietly, trying not to sound too mushy in front of the other guys. He was the sentimental, sensitive one of the three, and it was very touching. I smiled and nodded my head, fighting tears back. I'm transported back to the Cameroon rainforest every single time the shuffle on my phone surprises me with Frank Edwards's "This Love."

When I set back out into the heat and made my way in the direction I was shown, I noticed my backpack felt extra heavy again as I gingerly stepped with my tender feet. In less time than I anticipated, I spotted a lone car parked on the outskirts of town. A slender gentleman was sitting on its hood enjoying a cigarette in the sun. He saw me coming and gave a large wave of acknowledgement from afar to let me know I had made it. A huge rush of appreciation came over me as I was leaving Buea. My travel dates to Cameroon were completely random and flexible. What were the odds that I'd visit at a time when the president was making his first appearance in over a decade? It certainly had thrown a huge curve ball into my imaginary plans, and I suffered for it. But I wouldn't have changed a thing. Timing is everything, especially when you're in Africa. The unexpected is my favourite part.

"Hi, I'm Angela!" I said to the driver with enthusiasm. We both got into the car and settled into our seats. The gentleman was quiet for a moment, flicked his cigarette out the window and then looked over at me. "You sure have a pretty smile," he commented. *There you have it. Fergus, wherever you are, I'm officially out. But in the end I think I still won.*

KENYA

Approximately 6:30 p.m.

THAT EVENING, Samuel and I enjoyed a bowl of goat stew and noodles with the British military men. I loved listening to their fitness training stories, epic mountain adventures and innocent friendly banter. It was entertaining and educational at the same time. I learned that the British military often use Mount Kenya as a training ground for conditioning and mountaineering. It was also the night I was introduced to performing pull-ups off the top of a door. During the conversation, one of the guys challenged another gentleman to a pull-up showdown. They used the wooden front door of the refuge to compete. This, of course, led to everyone in the room eventually being encouraged (aka heckled) to participate.

When it was my turn, I knew the room had pretty low expectations, so I confidently walked over feeling very little pressure. I rose onto the tips of my toes to reach the top of the door and curled my fingers over. I bent my knees behind me to start in a dead hang (those were the rules) and I proceeded to pump out every last pull-up I had in my tired body. There was no holding back! I wasn't even close to first place...but I wasn't close to last either. (If I could add a wink emoji, I would right here.) My hands ached for days afterward, but it was totally worth it. Samuel sat next to me on the bench and patted me on the back. "See, I told you," he proudly told the group. "She is strong like a lion." Apparently, while I was reading in the bunk, there were discussions being held about how hard our day of hiking was. Samuel would never talk about himself, so he bragged about me instead while recounting our journey. I don't think being physically strong is what saved us that day though. I think Samuel's lack of ego and decision to hold off on going right away is what saved us. Anyone can muscle through something and hope for the best. Patiently waiting, even in terrible conditions, for the right moment: that's true strength. That was Samuel.

There weren't enough mattresses in the refuge for everyone, so I offered to share mine with Samuel. We both slipped into our individual sleeping bags and butted up against each other, similar to how we did on the mountainside. There were three other men in our room: one on the bunk above us, and two in the bunk beside us. All of them were sound asleep and snoring. "Anyela, are you sleeping?" Samuel whispered to me. "No. I'm very tired, but I cannot sleep," I answered back. "Me also," Samuel said. "Can you tell me a few more stories?" he asked again. "Yes, I am happy to," I responded back quietly. I could tell he had turned his head toward me from the crinkle of his sleeping bag. "Tomorrow will be a good day," he said very quietly. I knew it was his way of apologizing for the day, despite the weather conditions not being in his control or his fault. "Every day on the mountain is an adventure," I assured him. We both knew what I meant by that. The crinkle of his sleeping bag sounded again and there was a long pause. "I like that," he said in response. "So where are we going now?" he asked. "First to the Rwenzoris in Uganda, then to Malawi," I answered back.

UGANDA –
RWENZORIS

"**Y**ESSSSS.** I'm afraid you've picked a bad time to come. Lotsssss of rain. Lotsssss." The gentleman behind the small desk spoke with precise annunciation, paying particular attention to his S's.

I was standing in the middle of the Rwenzori Mountain Services Building (RMS is a nongovernmental, Indigenous organization that provides trekking support and services). It was nearly a ten-hour drive from the capital city of Kampala, and this was about the last way I wanted to be greeted.

"Is it possible to still trek the Rwenzoris, even with the rain?" I asked, desperately hoping for a yes. Of all the hikes in Africa, this was the one I was most excited about. It was considered to be one of the hardest hikes in the world due to the combination of high altitude, severe weather patterns and extremely muddy conditions. He stared at me with intense squinty eyes and a face so expressionless it was as if he had Botox injected everywhere. He pushed all of his fingertips together while his elbows rested on the weathered desk. The pauses between his sentences were intimidating and very confusing. I wasn't sure when he was finished his thought and when he was waiting for a response from me. After at least a full minute had passed while his eyes scanned me up and down, I went to speak up, until he finally did, cutting me off. "You've come all thisssss way, ssssso it isssss up to you (big exhale as he dramatically closed his eyes) to deccccide what you want to do. It isssss very wet."

I wasn't thrilled about the idea of spending the next five days in cold, damp conditions, but I had travelled for days to get here and expected that the weather, in these mountains in particular, wouldn't be particularly favourable. I read that this region can get up to three metres of rain a year and it is incredibly unpredictable; you never know how long the rain will last. I was about to respond, thinking he was finished again, but he continued his thought. "Terrible. Not good. Very wet." I awkwardly waited, unsure if he was finished. He blinked several times in a way that made it feel he was annoyed with me for not responding immediately. "Well, what isssss your anssssswer? I am waiting." He said it to me like I was the one with the communication problem. "I am fine with a little rain and cold. But will the conditions be safe for me to leave tomorrow?" I asked directly. There was an extra long pause from the gentleman, and a lot of blinking, but I resisted adding more into my window of opportunity to speak. "It'sssss hard to sssssay (long pause) because I cannot predict the weather (extra long pause). There may be a lot of rain; there may be a little rain. I cannot predict how you will walk in thessssse conditionsssss (brief pause). I do not know if you are sssssstrong, only you know if you are capable." He looked me up and down again as if he were judging for himself whether I could do it or not. I knew I was asking a question that was difficult to answer, because he indeed could not predict the weather, and he did not know anything about my ability, but there had to be a gauge to know what the safety level was at. I didn't know how to ask it any better than "Would you feel comfortable hiking the Rwenzoris tomorrow?" This was a dangerous question, because his ego could come into play, but it was all I had. He responded right away, which was a pleasant surprise and yet a little unnerving. "Yesssss. I think it isssss okay to go tomorrow." I didn't fully trust his answer, but it was the one I wanted so I went with it. I naively decided I'd go ahead with my plan to leave the next day, and if the weather really was too terrible, or the conditions were dangerous, I'd simply turn around. No biggie! It is amazing how we can twist details in our heads to find the solution that suits us best.

"Very good then. I will arrange the guide and a cook. You will alssssso require gum bootsssss," the gentleman explained. "I have hiking boots," I said while lifting up my foot to show him. He chuckled with amusement to himself and responded back, "Your expensssssive bootsssss are ussssselesssss for the Rwenzorisssss." He stepped out from behind his desk, directing me to follow him to the shed out the back of the RMS building. I couldn't help noticing he wore an oversized navy suit with the pant legs tucked inside green knee-high rubber boots. The mud was either no joke or this gentleman had an even worse fashion sense than me! I reluctantly followed him as he requested. I couldn't help thinking on the walk over that this was just a way to make more money. I was irritated with the suggestion, and the obligation I felt, but I wasn't in the mood to listen to him talk anymore. It would have likely been another half-hour before he explained himself.

Inside the dark, cluttered shed were piles of mismatched boots, random hiking poles, tattered coats and other hiking attire I assumed had been left behind by other trekking tourists. Several gentlemen searched for a pair of size eight rubber boots for me. There was one size eight for the right foot, but it had a huge hole in the side and its matching left was nowhere to be found. In the end, I was the recipient of one boot for my left foot that was a size nine and one that was a size seven for the right. I had zero expectations of using them, so I had no concerns about them being ill-fitting.

The next morning I met my guide, Sam. He was a slight man with very fine facial features. He spoke a little bit of English, very shyly, but had a confidence within him that I liked. He walked with purpose and it was obvious he was well conditioned. Right away I thought the two of us would jive really well.

The morning was sunny and hot, the exact opposite of what I arrived in and what I expected for the day. Sam commented on the weather and tried to make me feel comfortable about the conditions at higher elevation. "It will be a good climb. Maybe rain. But I think...it is good," he said reassuringly. I wanted to believe him wholeheartedly, but anyone that has spent any time in the mountains knows that weather can change rapidly. I wasn't fully convinced, mostly because I could tell he wasn't either. His ever-shifting eyes were a dead giveaway.

We sat next to each other on a large rock while we waited for some reason or another. I had no idea what was going on. A random gentleman I'd never seen before eventually approached us with a large satchel of food, along with three live chickens tied at the legs and banded at the beak. It was my understanding that the cook was already at camp one, but he was limited on supplies. Sam and I took on the responsibility of hauling the food and divided it up between our bags to share the load. It never occurred to me that I'd be asked to carry a live chicken under my arm as well. "Do not worry. He is friendly," Sam assured me with a smile. I named my little fella "Protein 1." I couldn't bear to give him a real name knowing what would happen to him in the very near future.

The weather was incredible, we had lots of food and Sam was great, but I still couldn't shake the nerves in my stomach. Despite the bad feeling, I slung my backpack on and took my first steps upward with my expensive and useless hiking boots to follow Sam, Protein 2 and Protein 3 into the Rwenzori jungle.

The entire morning of hiking couldn't have been more glorious. It might have been my imagination, but it even seemed like Protein 1 was having a good time. Every once in a while I'd look down at him under my arm and his little head would oscillate around in what I imagined to be curiosity. The mud trail was slippery from all of the rain, but it was very manageable. My positivity with regard to the trekking safety was improving with every switchback we rounded. After several hours of weaving in and around broken trees, fallen rocks and small landslides, Sam, all three chickens and I made it to our first camp. The day had been an easy steady climb yet very enjoyable. RMS had constructed refuge huts in strategic places for camping throughout the Rwenzori Mountains. The huts were wooden with green tin roofs that blended into the foliage. They were basic sheds that provided a dry place to sleep and were much more reliable than a tent at the rainy time of year.

Upon our arrival, I noticed a small man crouched over a stove just outside of the building, tucked under the tin roof overhang. Sam walked me over and introduced me to Calvin. He would be our cook for the next five days. He was astonishingly thin, almost sick looking, and his eyes, hidden behind crooked filmy glasses, did not focus in the same direction. I shook his hand to greet him and he smiled timidly. His hand was cold and felt weak. I noticed he was only wearing a T-shirt with a light oversized knit sweater over top. The sweater had numerous holes in it, making it appear as if it had been well used near open fire. He had leather sandals on and his suit pants were torn in several places. I didn't know it at the time, but this was all the gear he had with him. No coat, no boots, no rain gear. Since my coat was handy, I offered it to Calvin to warm up. He graciously shook his head no and went back to cooking. He was making chapatti and it smelled delicious. He clearly had done this before, but I was wary of his health and ability to trek for hours a day.

Later that evening I asked Sam about Calvin's condition. He assured me he wasn't sick and that he was a tiny man but strong. I'd seen this on prior trips – smaller gentlemen that were strong like hippopotamuses, so I decided I would take Sam at his word and not put limits on Calvin based on his frail appearance.

The next morning I abruptly woke up to the sound of rain crashing down on the tin roof. I didn't have any idea what time it was, but it was still completely dark outside. The sound was deafening and felt like a torture tactic or warning from Mother Nature. Sam and Calvin slept in another bunk across the otherwise unoccupied refuge. I loved the privacy, but it was a little disconcerting that there were absolutely no other people on the mountain. I knew this was not a popular trek to make in comparison to the famous Kilimanjaro, but I expected to see at least one or two hikers at camp.

Calvin prepared some eggs for the three of us. We sat on the damp wooden benches inside and tolerated the thunder of rain smashing into the metal above us. It was too loud to converse above it, so we sat with our own thoughts. Mine were primarily about Calvin and his lack of warm clothing. He was visibly shivering and refused my coat offer once again. I didn't want to be pushy about it, but I was genuinely worried about him that morning. I was so cold I sat erect on the bench fully clothed inside my sleeping bag. I unzipped the top half so I could use my arms to eat but kept the hood over my head so my back wasn't exposed to the chilly open room behind me.

Eventually, I had to climb out of my sleeping bag and pack it up for another day of hiking. I deliberately laced up my hiking boots again, feeling confident they would be superior to rubbers for traction and agility.

Prior to our departure, Calvin handed me a little plastic bag that contained a lunch he had prepared. A banana, juice box, two biscuits and a chicken sandwich with the crust cut off. It was explained to me that Calvin would pack up the stove, tidy the refuge and set out after us when he was ready. "Thank you, Calvin," I said with a smile. He seemed too nervous to speak, but he did give me a warm smile in return. I shook his slender hand and set off behind Sam into the pouring rain. I stopped midway up the first switchback when I noticed Sam had his two chickens in tow and I was empty-handed. "Protein 1! Sam, I forgot my little buddy!" I yelled out with surprising alarm. It was amazing how attached I'd become in just one day. Sam slowly turned around to face me. He had a look of distress on his face. "Anyela, Protein 1 is no more." I gave him the benefit of the doubt on his harshness, chalking it up to a second language thing. "We ate him for lunch," he added, making my forgiveness a little less easy.

The conditions were quickly becoming more slippery and our trail was a little narrower, a little less forgiving and increasingly dangerous. Because the rain had been falling for so many days prior, many trees had toppled down, covering the path. Some of the trees were so large in diameter the only option was to heave our bodies on top of them and slide over. Sam tossed Protein 2 and Protein 3 over like footballs, making me cringe. "I'll carry the chickens this time," I said to Sam, trying to spare them from another punt.

Several hours into our trek the rain started again, gradually intensifying. The poultry twins were now inside my extra large raincoat, being protected from the harsh pelting water. The hip belt of my backpack cinched my raincoat down so the chickens could nestle inside and not fall out the bottom. I left the top portion open so they had a little air. I'm sure I looked ridiculous, but it was a great solution to protect them and also free up my arms to crawl over trees with more ease. I'll admit the smell that came off of them wafted out the top of my coat and kind of grossed me out, not to sound like a diva.

(*Top*) First refuge, Mount Kenya.
(*Bottom*) Beautiful first day on Mount Kenya.

(*Top*) Lower Mount Kenya landscapes.
(*Bottom*) A view of Mount Kenya from the refuge.

(*Top*) The beginnings of a snowstorm, Mount Kenya.
(*Middle*) Navigating slippery rocks on Mount Kenya.
(*Bottom*) Crater Lake, Mount Kenya.

(*Top*) Friendly children, Tanzania.
(*Bottom*) View of Mount Kilimanjaro, Tanzania.

(*Top*) Mount Kilimanjaro Umbwe route trailhead, Tanzania.
(*Bottom*) Breakfast picnic on Mount Kilimanjaro, Tanzania.

(*Top*) Vegetation on Mount Kilimanjaro, Tanzania.
(*Bottom*) Scramble on Mount Kilimanjaro, Tanzania.

(*Top*) View of Mount Meru from Mount Kilimanjaro, Tanzania.
(*Middle*) Glacier on Mount Kilimanjaro, Tanzania.
(*Bottom*) Freezing sleeping conditions on Mount Kilimanjaro, Tanzania.

(*Top*) Mount Kilimanjaro summit, Tanzania.
(*Bottom*) Sunrise view from Mount Kilimanjaro summit, Tanzania.

(*Left*) A young gorilla, Bwindi Impenetrable Forest, Uganda.
(*Right*) Silverback gorilla, Bwindi Impenetrable Forest, Uganda.

(*Left*) Bushwhacking in the Bwindi Impenetrable Forest, Uganda.
(*Right*) Gorilla trackers, Bwindi Impenetrable Forest, Uganda.

(*Left*) Who said mountain trekking wasn't glamorous? Rwenzoris, Uganda.
(*Right*) Invaluable Gumboots, Rwenzoris, Uganda.

(*Left*) Miles of bog coming to an end, Rwenzoris, Uganda.
(*Right*) A short break from the rain, Rwenzoris, Uganda.

(*Left*) Rwenzori landscape, Uganda.
(*Right*) Rain creeping back, Rwenzoris, Uganda.

(*Left*) Wet conditions, Rwenzoris, Uganda.
(*Right*) Crater lake, Rwenzoris, Uganda.

(*Top*) Crater Lake, Rwenzoris, Uganda.
(*Middle*) A short reprieve from the rain, Rwenzoris, Uganda.
(*Bottom*) Rain in the Rwenzoris, Uganda.

(*Top*) Hot chapati, Rwenzoris, Uganda.
(*Middle*) Inside a refuge in the Rwenzoris, Uganda.
(*Bottom*) Protein 3, Rwenzoris, Uganda.

(*Top*) Everlasting flowers, Rwenzoris, Uganda.
(*Bottom*) Local rural transit, Uganda.

(*Top*) Underground church, Lalibela, Ethiopia.
(*Middle*) Simien Mountain views, Ethiopia.
(*Bottom*) Sunset over the Simien Mountains, Ethiopia.

(*Top*) Rural Ethiopian life.
(*Bottom*) Homemade barbell, Zanzibar, Tanzania.

(*Top*) Bumpy road to Virunga Mountains, Rwanda.
(*Middle*) Small village in the Virunga Mountains, Rwanda.
(*Bottom*) Dian Fossey Site, Rwanda.

(*Top*) Locals walking home from the market, Rwanda.
(*Bottom*) Shy, but curious little girl, Rwanda.

(*Top*) Vegetation in the Virunga Mountains, Rwanda.
(*Middle*) A glimpse of Mount Karisimbi before the clouds roll in,
Virunga Mountains, Rwanda.
(*Bottom*) Produce transportation, Rwanda.

(*Top*) A steady incline on Mount Cameroon.
(*Middle*) Loving the uphill climb on Mount Cameroon.
(*Bottom*) Fields of gold, Mount Cameroon.

(*Top*) The remains after a refuge fire, Mount Cameroon.
(*Bottom*) Foggy days, Mount Cameroon.

(*Top*) Walking on volcanic rock, Mount Cameroon.
(*Bottom*) Summit, Mount Cameroon.

(*Top*) Outside the Malawi gym.
(*Bottom*) Plaine des Sables, Réunion.

(*Top*) Erupting Piton de la Fournaise, Reunion.
(*Bottom*) Réunion Island forest, Réunion.

MADAGASCAR

(*Top*) Fishing at sunset, Madagascar.
(*Bottom*) Filling in the bridge gaps, Madagascar.

(*Top*) Curious kids, Madagascar.
(*Middle*) Rural life, Madagascar.
(*Bottom*) Rural transportation, Madagascar.

(*Top*) A birthday snorkel in the Indian Ocean, Madagascar.
(*Left*) A birthday lobster feast, Madagascar.
(*Right*) Homemade "37 Points" birthday cake, Madagascar.

(*Top*) Landscape surrounding Pic Boby, Madagascar.
(*Middle*) The road to Pic Boby, Madagascar.
(*Bottom*) Pic Boby region, Madagascar.

(*Top*) The infamous fertility waterfalls on Pic Boby, Madagascar.
(*Middle*) Iconic baobab trees, Madagascar.
(*Bottom*) Summit view from Pic Boby, Madagascar.

(*Top*) Pic Boby descent, Madagascar.
(*Bottom*) Final, glorious day on Pic Boby, Madagascar.

CONGO

(*Top*) One of many UN bases, Democratic Republic of the Congo.
(*Middle*) Water transport, Democratic Republic of the Congo.
(*Bottom*) Lava remains after Mount Nyiragongo 2002 eruption,
Democratic Republic of the Congo.

(*Top*) Inside the cauldron of Mount Nyiragongo, Democratic Republic of the Congo.
(*Bottom*) Summit approach, Mount Nyiragongo, Democratic Republic of the Congo.

We eventually reached a wide-open rocky area that became a host for much of the water flowing down the mountainside. A serious river had formed across the trail and it was being supplied with energy from the robust waterfall to our right. Sam seemed incredibly distressed, then turned to me and yelled over the rushing water, "We will cross here! It is the only way!" I had a thousand questions swarming in my head, but the main one was "How do you say HELL NO in Swahili?"

In preparation to die, we put on our rain pants and gaiters, then tightened the hoods of our jackets so only our faces were exposed. The chickens didn't like it, but it had to be done. They squirmed all over and tickled me, so I loosened the backpack on my shoulders to give them more space. It was also a precautionary measure in case I lost my footing and needed to remove it quickly to swim for safety. The slippery rock, the slope of the mountain and the strength of the water were all concerns for a major disaster. Not to mention, at the time, I didn't know how to swim and had a tremendous fear of water.

Sam turned to me with a "holy shit" face and directed me to hang onto him at all times as we walked forward. The water was rushing past so quickly it looked like a river you'd whitewater raft on, not walk through with poultry in your coat. I could visualize the consequences: one slip and we'd be taken down with the whitecaps and eventually approach the second waterfall that was about 50 metres to our left. With no rope, and 100 per cent trust, Sam stepped forward with my hand in his. We tentatively gripped our way along the slippery rocks toward the other side of the river about 30 metres away. The water was so cold and in some places it was more than waist deep. Sam continuously yelled at me over the powerful waves crashing on the rocks. "Hold on! Look forward! Don't look to the side! Slowly!" I most certainly wasn't going to look left! Left meant dead. I kept my focus on Sam's tuque and concentrated on every single lump under my feet. When Sam turned his head to the right, to calculate our directional path, I caught a glimpse of the terror on his face and it is forever embedded in my memory. I wish I could delete it, but every time I think of him – even years later – it's the first image that comes to me.

When we successfully navigated our way to the other side of the rushing water we both collapsed to the wet ground in fatigue and utter relief. It was hard enough to stabilize and not be dragged down by the whitecaps with just a backpack. I couldn't imagine how much more difficult it was with a *mzungu* (foreign person in Swahili) in tow. Sam was coughing and gasping for air while I felt like there was a spastic little critter trying to push through my ribs – that being my heart. (You were thinking I was going to say chicken, weren't you?) Well, the sensation did bring my attention back to them. I stood up abruptly and opened up my coat to check on my protein pets. Their little heads looked up at me, indicating they were oblivious and just fine. I, on the other hand, was a wreck, and couldn't help but wonder how many more of these river crossings we'd encounter. Spoiler alert: too many to remember.

My feet were completely soaked. My expensive useless boots lived up to their name and failed me. They were a bad purchase, unlike the silly mismatched gumboots! The rain was coming down much too hard to search in my bag for dry socks, so I took my wet boots and socks off and slipped my bare feet into the rubbers. My toes were scrunched up in the size seven, and the size nine left me with a floppy front piece that reminded me of a tongue as it slapped against the ground. *Well, this ought to add an extra element to the excitement.* I knew at least my feet would remain drier and this would prevent me from becoming even colder than I already was.

Sam gave me a thumbs up and we continued our trek in a matching set. I felt like a local poser, but Sam approved, so that made me feel a bit cooler. Up and up we went, but it wasn't as much fun as it could have been due to the wet conditions. This was typically my favourite type of terrain – a natural staircase made of rocks and roots. The soil beneath was clay-like, so when it became wet it was very greasy. I almost wanted to pull out my crampons to claw my way forward. There were several times when Sam would slip and then slide belly-down a steep slope and take me along with him. It was funny, as long as it didn't end with a boulder barricade, a branch jab in a not so nice place or a live chicken being flung. Protein 2 and 3 were on the adventure of their lives!

We walked for hours on the slippery ice-like conditions. It was two steps forward/one step back for most of it, making it twice the work it would be on a dry day. I signed up for this knowing the mud was a huge part of what made this journey so challenging. I had moments of regret; I'm not going to lie. The tediousness of it was frustrating and a new form of torture I'd not experienced before. The pummelling of the rain on top of it all was an extra special treat. This was a feat of mental strength more so than even physical.

Sam and I had to detour off the main path due to a landslide. We found ourselves on a narrow trail that had a thick wall of vegetation that brushed our left shoulders. To our right was a very thin line of trees that did a poor job of hiding a long drop toward an angry body of water. We both cautiously stepped along the thin path, grabbing random branches on the vegetation wall with our left hands for a feeling of security. One slip and it would be over. On the extra narrow section, Sam directed me to face the vegetation wall and shuffle sideways. This approach left room for my backpack and the opportunity to grasp onto the vegetation wall with two hands, instead of just one. I gingerly sidestepped in my ill-fitting boots and my bulging chicken-filled coat. (That's a sentence I never expected to write in my lifetime.) Inevitably, my size nine did not cooperate, causing me to lose my footing and slip off the edge of the trail. Everything was a blur. I couldn't focus on or hear anything. I was desperately holding onto a tree root with both hands; they were my only connection to my life at that point. I immediately went into survival mode. My hands were wet and the rain continued to pound down on us. I tried to put my feet up against something below to take some tension off my arms, but it was evident I was hanging in mid-air. There was no way Sam could help since the trail was so thin and he had his back toward me. One small wrong move and he'd be down too. I was alone in this. "Pull! Pull! Pull hard! You can do it! You are strong! Pull! Puuuuulll! Puuuuullll!" My ears reconnected with my brain and I could hear Sam screaming at me in terror.

After countless years of pull-ups at the gym, it was the day I hoped would never happen; the day I was forced to pull for my life. An unusual sense of calm came over me as I dropped my shoulder blades down my back like I would at the Derrick Club, and slowly elevated my body, bag and protein buddies up high enough to dig my left foot into the side of the trail overhang. (As I write this I'm shaking my head. What on earth was I doing with chickens inside my coat? I would never do that at home.) I simultaneously pulled with my arms and pushed with my foot to lift myself high enough to then push down with my hands to position my body back on top of the path. I crawled belly-down along the trail using my hands and the tips of my left toe, while my right foot wrapped around the edge of the trail to keep me from sliding sideways off the path. The chicken bulges in front of me, and my backpack behind, added an extra element of difficulty to an already crappy circumstance.

Once the ledge was wide enough, Sam was able to lend me a hand so I could stand up. He continued to hold my arm as he stared at me with tears slowly welling up in the inside corners of his eyes. I was too amped up to join him and I wasn't ready to talk about what had just happened or what could have happened. Instead, I made bad jokes about Protein 2 and Protein 3 being freeloaders and offering no help. When I opened up the zipper of my coat, only Protein 3 looked up this time. His buddy was lifeless, likely crushed under my body weight as I dragged myself to safety. I was devastated, but the shock I was in prevented me from reacting like I typically would. Rather than cry, I just stared at Sam with a look that could only say one thing: "I've got a dead chicken inside here." You might have to use your imagination for what that particular look is like; it's not one that comes up often. Sam took him from me and laid him inside the top of his bag. I knew his fate was coming, I just felt horrible being the one to have caused it.

I tried very hard to stay positive, but the relentless rain and mud on top of squishing Protein 2 were making it difficult. I didn't dare mention the thought of turning around, mostly because I didn't want to navigate the ledge again, but the conditions only seemed to be getting worse the further we walked.

Hours of slogging through the forest, slipping over tree roots and listening to the repetitive pounding of rain on my plastic coat became physically hard and an emotional drain. In the distance we could see the green roof of the next refuge. At first it was a beacon of hope, until it never appeared to get any closer. It was like a target that was forever moving away as we attempted to get near it. Eventually, the foliage hid our view (which was a blessing) as we plodded away to the finish line, not having to scrutinize our slow progress.

Upon our arrival at the refuge, we both unrolled our sleeping bags right away and switched out our clothes for dry ones. I wrapped Protein 3 in my sweater and placed him in the corner of my bunk. I was losing my mind a bit with the weather, the fatigue, the falling scare and the tragic end to Protein 2's life. Nurturing a chicken was a clear indicator of it. Sam checked in with me: "Anyela, are you okay?" Translation: "Not sure it's common in Canada, but here in Africa sleeping with chickens is a sign of crazy." "I'm okay Sam," I confirmed. Then the tears came down and I let it all out. "Just a scary day is all," I added. "It is very scary," he confirmed. "But it is okay now." He tried to comfort me with the few English words he knew. It worked. I wiggled into my bag and scrunched myself into the smallest ball I could in an effort to retain heat. No matter what I did, I simply could not warm up. I could see my breath inside the unheated building, and steam off my damp body.

There was one more added stress that wouldn't subside. I watched anxiously through the little window from my bunk for Calvin. I had a sick feeling of worry in my stomach that he wasn't okay. Sam and I had proper gear and we were suffering, so Calvin had to be in trouble. The weather was worse than any of us would have guessed. I awkwardly waddled over to Sam's bunk, still inside my sleeping bag, and asked permission for us both to gear back up and search for Calvin. He looked at his watch and decided it was a good idea. According to his timing, Calvin should have made it by now. The pit in my gut grew larger.

It was only three in the afternoon, but the dark cloud, torrential rain and nightmare of a day made it feel much later. We made our way back to the trail, slipping and sliding all over the place, trying to maintain traction and balance. Sam was out in front, while I followed. Within about 30 minutes we could see Calvin lying on the trail in the fetal position. It felt like an eternity to get to him. The slick path was similar to walking on an escalator going the wrong way, only the faster we tried to move, the worse our progress was. Sam yelled out Calvin's name in a panic. There was no response.

Eventually, when we reached him, Sam and I knelt on the ground immediately to check for vital signs. Calvin was no longer wearing his sweater, just the thin white T-shirt that was now stuck to him like Cling Wrap from the moisture, exposing every rib and vertebra in his body. I could feel a little breath on my cheek when I placed my head near his mouth, and there was a very slow rise and fall of his shoulder. "He's alive!" I yelled out to Sam. "He is still here? I will radio for help!" Sam announced with relief. He immediately called the RMS headquarters with his satellite phone to let it know our location. Calvin lifted his head a little but did not say anything. Sam and I were able to get him to stand and put one arm around each of our necks. Together we carried him to the refuge to wait for help.

Our elevation was too high for a decent fire to warm him, so we undressed Calvin from his saturated clothes and wrapped him in our sleeping bags. Calvin's teeth chattered and his body shook for some time. Eventually it stopped, making me feel even more nervous that his condition was worsening. I constantly checked his pulse to be sure we weren't losing him. Sam and I each took one of his hands to rub between our own in a desperate effort to warm them.

The sky was officially dark, this time due to the descent of the sun behind the mountainside, while the rain had thankfully slowed to a sprinkle. Three RMS rangers arrived at the refuge. Two of the men stood back while one checked on Calvin's condition. He was still alive but barely hanging on. Another ranger wrapped his limp body in the blankets he brought with him and lifted him onto both his shoulders. A satellite radio call was made (I'm assuming to RMS) to notify it of their departure. The men rushed out of the refuge, jogged up the trail Sam and I could barely walk earlier and disappeared within minutes. When I think about real-life superheroes, these guys are it.

This was now the second rescue I'd witnessed in just a few trips to Africa. The experience was another reminder of how vulnerable we are in the mountains.

That evening Sam received a call over his satellite phone to learn that Calvin and the three men had made it down safely. We were given the news that Calvin would recover. Relieved, I gave Sam a big hug and cried again after the scare was over. RMS gave us permission to continue the trek as long as we felt it was safe to do so. Sam and I both laughed at how "safe" the conditions were, but decided it couldn't get any worse going forward versus backtracking our previous steps.

Sam left the refuge for some time that evening, suggesting I rest a little while as he stepped out. I think both of us needed some quiet time alone. When he returned, he surprised me with a huge platter of food prepared by him. "It smells delicious Sam, thank you!" I said with appreciation as he handed me a plate, making no eye contact. I looked down to discover pasta, marinara sauce and a drumstick. "Protein 2?" I whispered. "Sorry Anyela," Sam whispered back. "He was good chicken," he continued, as if it were his funeral.

The next morning Sam and I sat together around the picnic table inside the refuge, nibbling on crumbly bread with near-frozen jam. The metal knife was so chilly it burned my hand when I tried to spread the strawberry preserves. We were both too tired and too cold to make anything more elaborate but knew we needed some energy for the long day ahead. The rain was still coming down but with less of a vengeance than the day before, making it a little more appealing. Our weather standards had become super low. While we packed our gear, Sam talked about the "Bigo Bog" we would encounter later in the day. "There will be many bogs today," he stated. I had walked through bogs at home, but I wasn't sure if we were on the same page about what a "bog" was. I envisioned spongy ground and tired legs because of it. "Your legs, they will get very tired," he continued, reinforcing what I was thinking. I nodded my head and asked, "We can do it Sam?" He smiled confidently. "Yes. We will do it." I needed that optimistic response more than he might have known. It was the answer I expected, and the reason I asked the question.

⊙ **"HURRFF,"** Sam grunted, following it up with something very long in Swahili that didn't sound too joyous. He grabbed hold of the stick I offered him. He was stuck, waist deep in mud, again. This was the Bigo Bog of the Rwenzoris. It was not the time to ask if this was "normal," or if we just happened to get lucky with a hiking condition nightmare...er, challenge. I was trying to stay positive with my thoughts. I've never done anything more difficult or frustrating in my life. Ever. At first glance it would appear we were inside a beautiful green valley at an altitude of around 4000 m, surrounded by glorious rugged peaks with ominous mist swirling between them. But with the rain vacillating between steady sprinklings and aggressive downpours we were actually navigating our way across kilometres of boggy misery, leaping between tussocks of grass trying to avoid falling and getting sucked into the earth. My mismatched gumboots impacted my coordination at times, causing several of my leaps to fail, resulting in messy lip stands. The mud was as deep as my chest in some regions, and then only as deep as my ankles in others. The unnerving part was that I couldn't tell which one I was about to fall into; everything looked the same to me. Most times it was an utter relief to miss the grassy mound I was aiming for and only land in mud above my boots. But every so often I'd miss and find myself chest deep, fully dependent on Sam to drag me out like a catfish. "Sam, if you were to trek this region by yourself and fall into one of these deep mud pots, how would you get out?" I asked, out of curiosity. "Impossible. You would die," he said definitively. "Okie dokie," I answered back, trying to lighten the vibe.

Clearly, Sam wasn't in the mood to gab. I understood; this required concentration and I was being a distraction. The truth was I needed a mental break from the agony of what we were enduring. Every single step required thought and precision, making the journey mentally exhausting, painfully slow and, with no consistent momentum, extra cold. It was a different kind of holiday. "Well, let's not both fall in at the same time then, okay partner?" I said jokingly. But then I thought about what I'd just said and began to ruminate over that disastrous scenario. *Think about something good, Ang. You're at the gym, it's back day, AND Dwayne Johnson walks in...and he's coming your way! And he has peanut butter!* How's that for a distraction?

I stood precariously on top of one of the grassy mounds and looked ahead. Thousands and thousands more surrounded us, making it feel like it would never end. I had an extra long leap to the nearest mound, so I swung my arms and went for it because there was no better option. My size nine boot caught on something and I plummeted chest first into the brown goo of death in front. It slowly sucked me down; only my backpack saved me from being fully immersed. Sam leaped backward carefully onto the mound I missed, leaned down and stretched out as far as he could to grab my hand. I couldn't reach and I was slowly submerging. In a panic, he handed me a stick and I was able to grab hold. He yanked me forward and dragged me belly down onto the grassy hill. I was so tired and fed up I started to laugh at the absurdity of what we were doing. My laughter escalated to a level where I was no longer making sound, mouth wide open, eyes shut, while my shoulders jiggled up and down. Sam suspected I was losing it earlier, but now it was official – I had gone mad. I went on for so long it eventually it became contagious. Sam fell to his knees in hysterics and rolled onto his back to try and catch his breath. Our sporadic gasps for air turned into grand howls that bounced off the mountain walls around us. I could feel Protein 3 wiggling around in my coat and it added fuel to the fire.

When we finally pulled ourselves together, I stood up to discover I only had one boot on. I pointed at my muddy foot and my convulsive laughter started up again. The mud had sucked my size nine right off! By the time we noticed, it was too late – the bog had swallowed it. I had to switch my remaining gumboot out for my expensive useless ones. For how annoyed I was at having to rent those gumboots, I was so sad to not have them anymore. The hissing man was right all along. I owed him a thank you, and an apology for my distrust.

The following days were a continuous mud grind, but the rain eased up just in time for us to make the final push to the summit. The last vertical climb with ropes and ladders was a welcome change of pace. It was the first time in days I felt like I was making forward progress at a natural speed. Sam and I stepped on top of the summit and sat for a moment to take it all in. The valley was incredible from above. The bogs looked so unassuming, almost majestic, while the crater lakes in the distance looked so tiny in comparison to when we walked past them. The clouds were still grey and thick, threatening more rain, but for our 20 minutes spent on the peak, they gifted us a break. If you were wondering, Protein 3 was indeed still in my coat. I don't know for sure, but he might be the first chicken to ever summit the Rwenzoris!

The descent was delightful in comparison to what we had been through the past few days. I finally had the ability to appreciate my surroundings instead of avoiding another mud fall. The silvery everlasting flowers, the giant lobelia and groundsel plants surrounding us made it feel like we were walking on another planet. Sam explained that some species of plants are only found in this particular region of the world. We both developed a hop in our step as we joyously bounded on rather solid ground among the rare, vibrant green and gold vegetation. The clouds ended their break and rain began to sprinkle down again. Puddles that would normally cause me to walk around them on a typical hike were no longer obstacles. I simply splashed through anything and everything! Being wet and filthy somehow became less crummy and more liberating. Our pace was picking up as we ventured down the valley. Sam and I were into a full-on jog. "Keep running!" Sam yelled back at me. "Run from the rain!" he added with a little giggle. I couldn't have agreed more. It felt so good to be moving, even if the rain was now pelting down hard again.

In the end, the escalating weather was the deciding factor to pass the last refuge and continue to RMS headquarters, making a two-day trip into one. The thought of being wet and frozen another night was not appealing to either of us. The day was long and exhausting but every bit worth it. It also spared Protein 3 his life (at least momentarily), since he was on the menu for the last refuge dinner.

Sam and I were welcomed back to the RMS headquarters with sun. We had our coats off, pants rolled up over our knees and Protein 3 was happily under my arm as we strutted in. It didn't even feel like we were in the same vicinity as the Rwenzoris.

The hissing man walked out to greet us right away. "SSSSSo. I undersssssstand it wasssss raining. I am ssssssorry for thisssss. It isssss...ssssso...unpredictable," he said as he looked down at my boots with disapproval. "The gumboots were essential. Thank you so much for suggesting them. I'm sorry I pushed back on the idea earlier," I admitted to him. "Where are they then?" he asked with a little skepticism. "I donated one to the bog, and the other is inside my backpack," I explained. "Hahaha. Ssssso it was a little bit wet," he responded without true understanding and a little mockery. It was infuriating to hear him minimize the conditions we had just endured. I felt like I had just won the battle of my life. "I thought to myself many times...it is impossible," Sam jumped in to clarify, obviously on the same page as me. I could have said so much, but I didn't have the energy to relive any of it. So instead I winked at Sam and retorted, "It was impossible, until it wasn't."

EPILOGUE

◎ **I WENT BACK AND FORTH** on adding this epilogue because the purpose of this book is to entertain, not deliver an educational lecture. But, after some thought, I decided it was important to tell the full story of Calvin, to bring light to the dangerous hiking conditions that many local African guides, porters and cooks endure. After years of travelling to Africa, Calvin is just one of many hiking professionals I've met who was inadequately equipped for the harsh mountain elements. Mountaineering gear is difficult to find in the larger cities, let alone in small communities. On the off chance waterproof jackets, down-filled coats, warm sleeping bags and socks are found, they are typically unaffordable. This leaves professionals to use whatever resources they have available, often making the trip more uncomfortable for them than it needs to be, or even fatal.

In Calvin's case, he did not recover like we were told when we had reached camp two. Because of his poor health prior (which was suspected) and his lack of appropriate gear, he died of hypothermia before the RMS team could get him down the mountain for further help. He was 31 years old. I believe the team kindly waited to give Sam and me the news after we returned, in an effort to make my experience a positive one. I can guarantee Sam and I would have turned around if we had been given the real report. Tourism is very important to the community and they want everyone to have a great experience so that more people will be enticed to visit. Unfortunately, in my case, the weather was horrendous, but that is no fault of theirs or an indication that it is like that all the time. There are many times of the year when you can visit with almost no rain! I can't even imagine it... so I'll have to go back and see it for myself.

If you or someone you know is planning a trip to Africa to hike mountains, please know that any gear donations are greatly appreciated and could literally save someone's life. After my time in the Rwenzoris, I now take extra items (listed below) to help these gentlemen (and a few ladies) protect themselves while they try to earn a living doing something that is terribly difficult in an effort to provide for their families.

Essential Gear List

1. waterproof raincoats
2. waterproof rain pants
3. warm socks
4. warm jackets
5. warm sweaters
6. warm sleeping bags
7. headlamps
8. sunglasses
9. warm gloves
10. balaclavas
11. warm hats/tuques
12. warm pants
13. thermal underwear/long johns
14. bags
15. water bottles
16. baseball caps (for the sun)

MALAWI

WHEN EXPLORING OTHER PARTS OF THE WORLD, trekking in the mountains is my first passion, but lifting weights in local gyms would be a close second. The gym environment, no matter what country you're in, is irresistible. I love to see how other people train – the exercises they repeat, the equipment (or lack thereof) they use and the music they select. The motivational posters on the walls (every gym has them), the banter between sets and the differing physiques between individuals and even cultures is fascinating! It's a wonderful way to immerse in local culture, meet new people and discover newfangled training techniques.

With the novelty and excitement comes a test of one's courage. Walking into a room full of people, stepping onto their home court, not knowing if you'll be accepted (especially if you're female) is intimidating. In some Muslim countries it's frowned upon or even prohibited for women to train in local gyms where male patrons are present.

◉ **NOVEMBER IN MALAWI** is smack dab in the middle of the rainy season. Naturally, I arrived in the capital city of Lilongwe with delusional intentions of trekking the slopes of Mount Mulanje at an altitude of 3002 metres in a torrential downpour. My horrendous experience in the Rwenzori Mountains had clearly not been enough to smarten me up! Thankfully, the park rangers at Mount Mulanje denied me access and insisted I wait until the weather cleared, for safety. (At least there was someone out there with some common sense.)

With time on my hands, I travelled outside of the hectic capital region to the city of Blantyre. I did self-guided walks through the muddy streets to discover what the area had to offer. Small shops with bread, fruit and nuts kept me occupied and fuelled between stops. After a full morning of exploring, I fortuitously stumbled across a local gym called the Sweating Room. It was a hole-in-the-wall place that could not have been more than 800 square feet. The yellow painted concrete and colourful inspirational messages on the outside walls (in English) drew my attention right away. "Sweat Everyday." "No Pain No Gain." "Love Your Body." As I walked closer to see if it was open, I could hear the banging and clanging of weights between music beats, confirming it was. I had no idea what the protocols were, or who was allowed to train at this gym, but I was determined to find out. I knew that Malawi wasn't predominantly Muslim, so my chances as a female to join in were a little better.

I stood at the open entryway, which was partially covered by a thin flowered bedsheet, to take in the scene. There was a large cracked mirror on one wall that consumed everyone's attention, which conveniently gave me time to look around without being noticed. There were corroded mismatched dumbbells strewn all over the dirt floor, four dishevelled heavy bags hanging in each corner, several homemade barbells made with sticks and paint cans filled with something heavy looking, three benches – each held together with tape and cardboard – and numerous local gentlemen of all ages who looked like they could bench press a truck (or two). There was distorted reggae music pounding out of an old-school radio thanks to a wire signal antenna meticulously strewn through the cracks in the concrete wall. The lack of airflow made for extra heat, and the combination of rain and sweat seemed to have increased the humidity. The whole place smelled like a gym bag filled with wet T-shirts and socks.

It was filthy and intimidating, but I couldn't have been more delighted to discover the place. I pulled my shoulders back, took a few deep breaths and contemplated stepping inside, desperately hoping I could walk in without drawing too much attention. I could feel my heart beat in my throat and ears. It was reminiscent of the sensations and questions I had years ago, moments before leaping off the bungee jump platform. *Is this a good idea? Is this safe?* I had many reservations and uncertainties, but the only way to get answers was to take two steps inside. So I did.

Whoosh! Every single head in the room turned collectively, and all eyes were on me within seconds. I stopped dead in my tracks and gulped air because I had no saliva left. If it weren't for the music, I'm certain you could have heard my wet feet squish inside my shoes and every blink of disbelief in the room. One guy didn't even bring his arms down from his shoulder press. He just stood there holding ginormous weights above his head as he stared, mouth wide open. I couldn't sense what anyone was thinking because each face was frozen. I was incredibly paranoid I had just intruded and wasn't welcome. My flight response was signalling me to run from the testosterone jungle and avoid all discomfort at once. The only thing that kept me there was the knowledge that the hard part was over. I owed it to myself to at least ask if I could use the facility to train. The worst that could happen would be to hear "no," and then to embarrassingly retreat in rejection.

I nervously and very un-cool-ly waved to the group and smiled in an attempt to show friendliness. I didn't speak the local language, so I relied on my lame, unnatural and exaggerated gestures to get my point across. I pointed to the dumbbells on the floor and then back to myself, then back to the dumbbells one more time. Unfortunately, I was the only one who seemed to think my hand gestures were making sense. I received no response, just more blinking. Next, I'm embarrassed to admit that I flexed my arm and then pointed to the dumbbells, hoping that would make things crystal clear. Nada. Crickets. I just made myself look like a fool. In a panic, my last resort was to display a few dollars to show I didn't enter by mistake and had full intentions of paying to use the gym. I should have known all along, money talks. A young jacked dude in a tight tracksuit swaggered toward me and accepted my cash after the initial shock of what he'd witnessed had subsided. He nodded his head sideways to indicate I could go ahead with my workout. I was in!

Suddenly, everything I was wearing, holding and doing with my arms felt super awkward. My knees didn't want to bend like I wanted them to, causing my gait to go wonky while I made my way to the nearest corner to collect myself and dispose of my bag of groceries. I could feel the crowd's eyes unapologetically glaring as I navigated my way around the room to find something I was confident I could lift. It was tricky! The dumbbells were unmarked and corroded to the point that they were misshaped. Despite having spent the majority of my free time in gyms the past 15 years, I was feeling pressured to prove myself and earn a slice of their lifting real estate. In my mind the first dumbbell I selected was going to set the tone for how these dudes perceived me. They were all eagerly waiting.

If I picked something up that was too heavy, and I tragically failed, I'd look like I didn't know what I was doing. If I picked up something that was really light, it would confirm everything I assumed they were already thinking: she has no business being in our manly dude cave. There was a lot on the line and my fitness ego cared a great deal about the outcome.

I wrapped my hand around a lone dumbbell that had a huge chunk broken off one side. I guessed it to be around 45 pounds in its original state and subtracted five pounds to compensate for the missing section. My arms and back weren't prepared for the unexpected heaviness as I struggled to pull it off the ground. It felt like 100 pounds! I'd like to point out that it's not easy to pick something up when you anticipate it to be a certain weight and discover you were incredibly wrong. *Hot damn, what's this thing made of? Well, you're not shoulder pressing this lady! Think of a plan B, quick!* My game plan took a dramatic detour when I found myself having to use my legs to even get the dumbbell off the floor. I couldn't do anything with that kind of weight using just my arms, so I moved straight into a goblet squat to make it look like it was my plan all along. *Seamless. Don't make eye contact, just move this thing as smoothly as you can so it looks like it was the natural choice.*

I slowly moved up and down through my repetitions while simultaneously calculating my next move and scanning the weights around me for potential lifting options. Everything was a mystery. Dumbbells that looked like monsters weren't as heavy as I thought they would be, and others felt like they would tear my arm off. I was playing dumbbell roulette with a full audience chattering behind me in a language I didn't understand. I felt foolish but hung onto the fact that I knew what I was doing. I just needed some time to figure out the equipment. Besides, I already had that delightful addictive muscle pump going, so I wasn't planning to leave anytime soon. My legs and glutes got more of a workout initially because I was too proud to pick up a dumbbell and then put it down in shame when I discovered its true weight. My rule became "you pick it up, you lift it – some way, some how."

With a lot of trial and error I eventually found my groove and was navigating the tiny gym to the best of my newfound knowledge. Discovering that the "lighter" dumbbells were the ones with fewer chunks broken off was a big win. I guessed that those dumbbells were likely not used as often, dropped fewer times and abused less. With my new understanding, I was able to get down to business with a much more organized routine. I spent about 45 minutes getting my bearings and another 90 minutes doing what I love. It was a day and dollar well spent, despite the discomfort of having an audience – one that was growing very quickly. I wasn't sure if it was simply the time of day, or if word was spreading around town that there was a crazy foreign lady lifting things at the Sweating Room. There were 13 of us shoulder to shoulder in front of the foggy mirror and at least 30 more fellas behind us. It was a packed house! The pink cotton tank top I was wearing had blotches of sweat on it and my hair was dripping bullets of bliss. My body felt properly shredded, so it was time to call it a "workout complete" and grab my bags.

Kneeling down in the corner, collecting my things in preparation to leave, I heard a stern voice behind me: "I want to train." I turned around to find a six-foot-tall human musculoskeletal model hovering over me. His traps looked like black mountains hovering above two huge solid boulders that were his deltoids. He was clean cut with a shaved head, dark brown eyes and a smile almost as bright as his florescent yellow tank top. I was confused and a little awestruck while he stood rather close, looking down at me. It was the first time anyone in the room had spoken directly to me. Sadly, this was my awkward response: "You want to train? That is nice. (Duh.) That will be fun." *Oh Ang, really? Could you be any less cool right now? Well, no, obviously!*

Luckily, it didn't appear that the Adonis before me understood anything I was saying. He simply smiled and set two dumbbells down next to me. *Is this a parting gift? Am I supposed to clean these?* I had no idea what was happening. A huge toothy white smile grew on his face and his eyes widened like he was getting excited about something. "Front of the arms and back of the arms!" he announced with a very deep voice. "That is nice. That will be very nice." My response confirmed I actually could be even less cool than I thought. He leaned down and squeezed my arm and then guided me to stand. *What is happening right now? Am I in trouble? I paid.* The language barrier was clearly frustrating him too, so he was resorting to physical contact to get his point across. *Wait. Does he want me to work out with him?* I couldn't imagine a reason why, other than perhaps he was a personal trainer and wanted me to hire him.

I attempted to get clarification and tried to communicate that I had no more cash on me, but he wasn't interested in talking. He put the dumbbells in my hands and then grabbed a set for himself. I was clearly doing this with him and I had no clue what was in store. I followed him back to the mirror and all the men in front shifted over to make room for us. "You start. Front of the arms," he spoke sternly, likely more so than he would have in his own language. I slowly lifted my arms methodically to isolate my biceps. He watched and smiled in approval, then followed along at the same pace. Relief came over me when it became clear he didn't want to train me after all; he wanted a training partner! *What is happening right now? Why does he want to train with me? This is so weird...and SO AWESOME. Stay cool. Stay cool. Less smiling. Try to blend in.* My only suspicion was that he was doing this because I was a novelty and it would be a good story for later. The irony wasn't lost on me.

Between our first two sets I discovered my new workout partner was named Obadiah. With his girth, he could stand in front of me and I'd disappear. It was obvious all the guys revered him but shared the same sense of intimidation I had. Obadiah had two distinct sides: his hardcore-I-could-tear-you-in-half-focused-game-seven-all-in-training side, and his friendly complimentary-smiling side. Mostly he was dialled into side one, but between sets side two came out and it made me feel a little less fearful of death by training.

Obadiah had a passion for bicep exercises, so we did every single version you could think of, with vigour! He had to spot me at the end because the connection between my brain and muscles literally felt broken. He stood directly in front of me and gently guided my hands up as he hollered out motivational messages. "You look soooo goood. You are very strooong. I love your boooody." He would dispute it, but I'm pretty certain he was doing the majority of the lifting at that point in time. I had to hold back laughter because my arms simply weren't cooperating and Obadiah seemed to think it was the greatest thing he'd ever seen. There was no way he could have been impressed with the weight I was lifting, but perhaps he was with my perseverance. Or maybe he just had super low expectations and the fact that I was even lifting weights flabbergasted him! It certainly wasn't common for ladies to exercise in this region, let alone lift weights at the gym.

Next on the never-ending-arm-shred agenda, we moved on to another 60 minutes of tricep work. It was daunting not knowing how long the training session was going to last. I wanted to perform to the best of my ability, but I also felt the urge to pace myself with how much I was lifting in case we had hours more to go. I wasn't sure how much more my arms could tolerate, but my ego was still on par with Obadiah – it wasn't showing signs of slowing down anytime soon. At one point I was instructed to stand on his back, with a large plate in tow, while he completed his tricep push-ups. The entire time I was balancing on his bulging lats I was considering how I could avoid this for myself. Luckily, he didn't broach the idea of standing on me. I was giddy with relief when all he wanted to use was the plate on my back. That was certainly an exercise in perspective! I believe a miracle happened that day because somehow I was able to push through my already shredded triceps and not fall on my face during the execution. I am still forever grateful but unsure of how I did it without ripping something.

Hours into the workout our conversation between sets became limited to grunting, profanities and very short statements. I had to concentrate so hard on what I was doing I literally couldn't speak most of the time. Occasionally, we'd make eye contact to acknowledge mutual pain and respect. My tank top was saturated in sweat and clung to my body, leaving nothing to the imagination. I kept wringing it out and moving it away from my skin as best as I could. "You could take it off! Be free!" Obadiah suggested. "Ah, it's okay. Thank you," I said sheepishly. Although it would have been so much more comfortable, I didn't need to draw any more attention than I already had. The guys were all obsessed with touching each other's abs. Between sets they'd walk around and pat each other on the stomach in appreciation for their hard work. I knew I was officially accepted when they felt comfortable enough to do the same to me.

Just when I thought we had covered every aspect of our arms, Obadiah decided to "finish" the workout with some more biceps. No, I'm not kidding. Believe me, I wouldn't joke about that. He handed me a barbell and we curled until we could curl no more. Obadiah openly admitted he was in discomfort as we finished things off. It was so validating to know I wasn't alone! "Oh my gawd, my arms are hurrrrting! I loooove biiiiceps!" His voice sounded like thunder as he slowly reefed the metal up methodically. If you're wondering, no, my cool factor never did kick in. Like a true Canadian, I managed to grunt out, "You. Sure. Liiiike. Them. Eeeehhhh? If Iiiii die, Iiiii'm soooory."

Simultaneously, Obadiah and I set the barbells down and collapsed flat out on our backs in utter exhaustion and euphoria. I didn't care that the dirt would stick to me. I didn't care that dudes were walking around our heads. I didn't care that my arms wouldn't extend. It was all worth it. "What is happening? What is happening?" Obadiah said with a giggle as he noticed his arms, too, did not extend all the way to the ground. As a fitness trainer I'm not suggesting this is ideal. It's actually really stupid. Obadiah knew it was too. But sometimes it's just kind of fun to do stupid things.

I'm not sure who had more fun that afternoon. No matter where you are in the world, you can always find someone in the gym that loves fitness as much as you do. I was so delighted Obadiah saw that in me.

We eventually peeled ourselves off the floor and I collected my things to leave. I'd been in the Sweating Room for almost five hours! Obadiah walked me out to the courtyard in the front of the building and pointed to a local lady grilling chicken over a fire. There was a lineup of fellow weightlifters anxiously waiting for their post-workout protein. *This is the Malawi version of our smoothie bars back home. This is so cool!* Obadiah treated me to a chicken. Yes, you read that correctly. I had an *entire* chicken to myself. It was five hours of training, okay! I actually had very little appetite, but there was absolutely no way I was going to miss out on the experience or refuse Obadiah's kind offer.

The rain had passed and the sun was slowly peeking through the clouds. Obadiah and I sat on a couple of large rocks while we pulled meat off the bones with our fingers and teeth, observing the fellas around us conversing in the local language. I wished so much I spoke Chewa so I could have understood what they were talking about. From their flexing actions, it was clear they were discussing training, and perhaps gloating about their lifting. In many ways, it felt just like home.

Every once in a while, Obadiah would check in with me and see if I was enjoying the chicken. "You like it? Is it okay?" He was so kind to be sure I was feeling comfortable with the food, and perhaps the male-dominated environment as well. The testosterone was almost greater outside the gym than even inside. Perhaps it was the post-workout energy. I assured him I was enjoying my time very much and then displayed my meatless bones as evidence. He smiled with satisfaction and then squeezed my shoulder and gave me a thumbs up, indicating it was good for our training. We sat quietly as we digested and enjoyed the shenanigans we were watching around us. It was pure entertainment with guys comparing six packs, having push-up competitions and comparing bicep girth. Obadiah didn't seem to want to join in, but I had the sense he wouldn't have even if I were not there. He didn't have anything to prove; he knew he was the best of them. Everyone knew.

The clouds slowly rolled back in and they became my cue to start heading back to my hostel. I thanked Obadiah for the epic day and tried my very best to express just how much I loved it. He giggled about how he still couldn't extend his arms and then looked down at mine and noticed I was inflicted with the same condition. "You did this to me!" I joked with a smile. "I did. It will help you remember Obadiah," he said with his infectious grin.

The Malawi Adonis, as I refer to him now, might not have intended for his final words to have such a lasting impact. It's been more than half a decade, countless curls later, and I can still hear that intimidating and motivating voice: "The buuuurn is so good. Very nice flexing. The flex is good!"

KENYA

Approximately 7:00 a.m.

THE SUN MADE A VERY WELCOME APPEARANCE the next morning. Overnight the sky gradually turned from a deep depressing grey to a vibrant energizing blue. The military men were up early and only minutes away from departure when Samuel and I stepped out of the bunkroom into the common area. We wished the men good luck and a great day of climbing. It was amazing how the scenery had changed around the refuge from a bleak wetland with no visibility to a glorious crystal clear view of the snowcapped Batian, Nelion and Point Lenana peaks of Mount Kenya.

Before we began our final day of descent, we decided to take advantage of the sun and dry out our gear. We climbed on top of a large boulder outside the refuge and laid everything we had out on its surface. We both stretched out our legs and looked up at the sun to get a little on our faces. "Where to next?" Samuel asked, catching me by surprise once again. He didn't need a distraction this time, so this request was clearly out of curiosity. "Well, let's see. How does a volcano in Réunion sound?" I asked with a grin. "Where is that?" Samuel asked, shaking his head like I'd made it up. "It's an island in the Indian Ocean," I explained.

"Okay, please tell me about this place," he said while he lay down beside me on the rock surface and closed his eyes. "Okay, first we'll visit Réunion, and then we'll head to Madagascar. It's right next door," I said.

RÉUNION

IT WAS 3:00 A.M. I was wide awake and ready to shake in Réunion! The exotic island, tucked off the east coast of mainland Africa, has been described as the "Amazonian Himalayas" and is a mecca for hiking. I stepped into the little rickety tin box that was my rental car and began my journey to find the base of a popular volcano (Piton de la Fournaise). My early departure was intended to give me enough time to make the drive (with a little wiggle room to compensate for any wrong turns), and then hike to the summit to see the sunrise. It was my final day in Réunion and this was the only volcano I had not stepped foot on yet. I was excited to round off my three-week adventure with one final scramble and one epic view.

There were no maps or GPS units available in the capital city of Saint-Denis due to the national holiday and an influx of visitors. Had I been organized like everyone else seemed to be, I might not have missed out on these useful items. Instead, I was relying heavily on MapQuest's detailed list of 199 steps on how to get to the base of Piton de la Fournaise. I'd like to say that my number was an exaggeration, but it really was 199. Initially, I thought the detail would be advantageous, but it turned out driving a stick shift for the first time in 15 years, in the dark, through winding mountain roads, in a country where all signs were in French (which I did not speak), in conjunction with attempting to interpret and follow the steps correctly, proved to be a tremendous challenge.

I made my way through the city and onto the freeway, feeling really good about my timing. I knew it wasn't a guarantee, but I wanted to give myself the best chance I possibly could to arrive at Piton de la Fournaise before the cloud and fog crept in to obstruct my view.

I took my exit off the freeway and the real navigating began. I headed into the forest and began to steadily climb. My little car chugged along the smooth road, often only in first or second gear to make the steep hairpin turns without stalling. Luckily, there were very few vehicles on the road at that hour, so I could crawl along a little slower to read my next step and then follow the "slight turn" or "hard left" that was indicated. MapQuest guesstimated it would take just over two hours to drive to my destination. I was already one and a half hours in and nothing around me looked hikeable, making me question whether I had missed a critical turn. Stubbornly, I continued to drive for ten minutes more, eventually finding a long enough stretch of road that made it safe to turn around. I ventured back and took a right turn that felt "correct," and followed the road for about 30 minutes until the MapQuest directions began to misalign with what I was seeing. Frustrated, I swivelled the car around again and drove back to the main road. I went even further this time and took another "correct-feeling" right-hand turn, convincing myself it was obviously the one. It was not.

At nearly 6:00 a.m. the sun was up. I'd missed my wishful view of the sunrise from the summit. *This wasn't the plan!* I was inappropriately baffled that my weak plan didn't work out the way I had envisioned it. Bullheadedly, I kept trialing the same roads over and over, hoping the directions would miraculously line up, but they never did. My frustration built to a high enough level that I needed to pull the car over and have a moment (it was actually a spaz). I was so mad at myself! I felt like an absolute fool driving around and around using my "gut instinct" that was obviously clueless. It was reminiscent of the film *A Nightmare on Elm Street*, when the kids were driving in the same circle, going nowhere, until Freddy Krueger could find them! On previous travel escapades, I'd always been fortunate to meet a local kind enough to guide me in the right direction. This time, I was completely on my own and it was eye opening. There wasn't a Freddy anywhere!

Clouds rolled in and shortly after rain began to spit down on the windshield. With my confidence cracked, in addition to the escalating rain, I was beginning to feel like my time was up. Ninety per cent of the music on the radio was French pop songs, but the remaining 10 per cent was in English. I made a deal with myself that if the next song played were to be in English, I'd keep trying for one more hour. If the song were in French, I'd end the insanity I was living. It was a commercial break. "Seriously?" I said out loud. While I sat and waited impatiently for the deciding song, a sick feeling came over me while thinking I might go back to Canada having to relive every turn on the road as the "possible one" that I should have tried. The commercial break ended and the next song came through with surprisingly clear reception. I turned the key over and slowly rolled back to the main road, weeping to the French power ballad. Of course, it had to be a sad song! *Okay, loud and clear! It's time to go home. Time to end this madness.*

It was 10:00 a.m. when I reached the main freeway leading back to Saint-Denis. If you're like me when I read, you're calculating how many hours I was driving around in circles for. I'll save you the effort: it was seven hours (minus a few minutes to pout). It's fitting that I was born in May and am a Taurus. I'm about as stubborn a bull as they come.

My stomach felt sick with regret but also hunger. I hadn't eaten anything all morning, so I planned to take the earliest exit and improve my day with a nice breakfast. I parked the car and walked into a lovely French bakery. Even the smell of fresh bread wasn't enough to cheer me up quite yet. I didn't want my last hours in Réunion to end on a sad note, so I planned in my head what I was going to do about it. *First, I'll have a picnic in the car, and then what? Ha! I'll go to a gym!* I was all set with a game plan and ready to turn my attitude and day around.

The gentleman behind the counter handed me the quiche I picked out and pointed me in the direction of where to pay. I walked over and handed my coins to the lady at the till. As we made the exchange, I could see a newspaper over her shoulder with a chilling image of a volcano erupting. Lava was spewing out like fireworks and fissures were oozing with red fire. I couldn't remember the word for "today" in French, so I used *lundi* (Monday), hoping she would understand the question I had in my head. *Is Piton de la Fournaise actually erupting today? Right now?* I kept my eyes on the newspaper behind her in hopes it would direct her to turn around and put two and two together. She looked over, then back at me and responded, "*Oui!*"

One word was all it took to re-inspire me. I was going back up there!

I sat on the hood of my little car and ate my French delight as the rain slowed and the sun began to peek through the clouds. I reviewed my MapQuest directions and crossed off the sections I had already covered so I could follow them more easily while driving. I still didn't have a solid plan, and it wasn't obvious where I'd gone wrong earlier, but I was ready to try one more time. The volcano was erupting, how could I not?

I drove back onto the freeway, took the familiar exit and navigated the road through the forest one more time. I found a familiar turn I had tested twice: sometime around 4:30 a.m. and then again around spaz time. For whatever reason, my gut was telling me it was the one to trust. I took a hard left and never looked back. The road didn't quite match the directions on my page, but I knew I only had enough time to commit to this one option now. I had to catch a flight back to Canada at 11:00 p.m., which meant I had to find the base of the volcano, hike up, hike down, drive back to Saint-Denis to collect my bag, drop off the rental car and taxi to the airport to be there three hours in advance – all in less than ten hours. No pressure.

Farmland transitioned to forest, which gave me a little glimmer of hope that I was travelling in the right direction up the volcano. Tall, lush trees lined the continuous inclining road. Eventually, they thinned out and I was able to see the horizon. I still wasn't certain I was headed in the right direction, but I kept going anyway, ignoring the contradictory voice in my head holding out for some kind of confirmation sign. *"Piton de la Fournaise, turn right, or one kilometre"* would have been nice. *Is that too much to ask, Réunion?*

The little car rattled up the road with determination, and a familiar voice came on the radio. It was Jason Derulo singing his hit song "Want To Want Me." *An English song! This has to be the right way! Obviously.* Clearly, I had actually gone insane with my previous seven-hour gong show because *this* was what I used as my sign. It's quite sad how much comfort it gave me, and, even worse, how often I've relied on Jason's powerful lyrics to calm me at home since. They're powerful stuff.

The landscape abruptly changed and the terrain turned into an ominous moonscape. My tiny car made chugging noises as I pushed on and off the gas pedal to twist and turn through the unusual fine black stones beneath the wheels. I assumed this was the Plaine des Sables I had read about. In my travel book it was described as a mysterious-looking landscape incapable of growing vegetation due to the high acidity of the volcanic land. To add to the eeriness, clouds rolled in again and rain pelted down, making the drive that much more challenging. It certainly wasn't favourable hiking weather, but I decided to keep going anyway. The purpose of the adventure had quickly shifted toward overriding my previous failure and simply finding the trailhead. My expectations had comically changed from "glorious private hike with unobstructed sunrise views" to "let's just find the damn thing."

Rain poured down faster than the windshield wipers could keep up with, leaving me no option but to pull off the trail for about 30 minutes for safety. The radio was no longer working due to the remoteness of the area, so I closed my eyes and listened to the constant hammering of the water on the metal roof. I had never felt more alone in my life. I was a small speck of faded red metal amid a vast black valley. From above, it would likely appear I had lost my way, which was still a very good possibility. I hummed Jason Derulo ever so pathetically just to feel a little hope.

Surprisingly, the rain slowed dramatically. I pushed the clutch in and started the car back up and puttered along the rocky rutted path toward who knows what. I had given up on MapQuest hours ago and was relying on my suspicions solely at that point. It was a scary time.

Then, out from behind a towering mound of black rock, came two vehicles with bright headlights driving in my direction. I slowly passed the other vehicles, attempting to see what the passengers were wearing. It appeared to be outdoor gear; perhaps something one would wear hiking. This could only mean two things: I was either in the right place or the wrong place. My spirits lifted and my heart began to race in anticipation of what might be ahead. I was still steadily climbing and periodically passing more vehicles, which reinforced my confidence. The path appeared to continue further, but there was a parking lot filled with several cars, which I suspected was where I needed to go. I pulled over and noticed signs (real wooden signs) with drawings of a volcano on them. There was still no formal signage (that I saw, anyway) with the words "Piton de la Fournaise," but I figured this had to be it. The few people in the parking lot were removing their rain gear that would have been essential just 20 minutes prior, but now the sun was shining, radically improving the temperature and the overall mood of the location.

It was almost 2:00 p.m. and I had no clue how long the hike would take, so I decided it was best to run it in an effort to maximize my time. I swapped my hiking boots for runners, tied my coat around my waist in case the weather opted for yet another change, tucked my earbuds into my iPod and grabbed my camera. It was go time!

The terrain started off fairly rocky, causing me to take it slower than I wanted in an effort to avoid an ankle sprain. Gradually, I made my way through the flat area and up toward the rolling mounds of scree and small shrubs ahead. The path became quite defined and I discovered my first sign (another real wooden one) affirming my Nikes were planted on the correct volcano. *I did it! I DID IT! I'm not a total idiot!* If I had to turn around at that time, it honestly would have been enough satisfaction for me. After all the uncertainty and self-doubt I'd endured the previous 11 hours, I was just thrilled to have persevered and found my way. Luckily, I still had time, so I was able to continue on. It was so much easier to do so, knowing it was the right way.

The trail gently switched back and forth through small gnarled trees and various colours of heather. The sun was hot, causing my skin to turn a little pink. Sweat was soaking through my tank top and my heart was racing with joy as I veered around each corner of the path, hopping over the odd root or rock lying in the way. My quads and calves burned, only easing up when I came to a full-on stop to process what I could see happening in the distance.

There it was, Piton de la Fournaise's cauldron coughing up continuous reddish-orange lava. I took a few photos and then continued to run as close as I could to the natural phenomenon. Eventually, I reached a fence blocking the path.

I sat on a ledge overlooking a deep valley with a great view of the eruption just on the other side. Silvery-coloured heather surrounded me, making it feel like I had the entire place to myself. I took my earbuds out so I could listen to the roar of the lava and the sporadic cracks of fire, which created a glorious light show. I didn't have a lot of time to stay, but I was appreciative of every minute I had. Just before I was about to leave, I put my earbuds back in and played Jason's song while I watched the spectacular eruption before me. It just felt like the right thing to do.

EPILOGUE

◎ **WITH EVERY ADVENTURE** I learn something new. This one was an eye-opener on just how vulnerable I am when travelling alone. I never had the opportunity to rely on anyone else, and subconsciously I think it weakened my confidence after every wrong turn I made. I don't believe it was an accident I walked into that bakery and saw the newspaper, though. I was given a second chance, one I could have easily not taken – for a variety of reasons. But because I did, this is the adventure I'm most proud of.

MADAGASCAR

CHAOS IS THE ONLY WAY TO DESCRIBE the traffic in the capital city, Antananarivo. Hundreds of cars, trucks and transport vehicles; cattle with carts; goats and chickens; people on motorbikes, bicycles, in wheelchairs, on horses, and almost everyone with various things in tow – appliances, produce, other people, mattresses, furniture, more animals, clothing, you name it! Dust and debris flew everywhere. Kids picked through piles of trash in bare feet, men sat in large groups and smoked and an endless ageless group of people touted random items like corn on the cob, magazines, hairbrushes, mops and candy as they meandered between cluttered, unorganized "lanes" of traffic. It was madness and it conjured up an array of questions and emotions I couldn't express to the driver due to the language barrier. My eyes scanned the flurry of activity before me and tried to make sense of what I was seeing. From a naive visitor perspective it felt like there were no rules, no regulations and no consequences. Pickup trucks filled with at least 100 kids in the back, toddlers carrying machetes as they scurried behind their mothers, huge open fires burning random items seemingly unattended, pedal bikes transporting dead goats, shirtless and shoeless men wandering the hectic roads carrying multiple cases of cola on the tops of their heads, and the disorderly stick scaffolding supporting workers multiple stories above ground are images tattooed in my memory when I think back to my time there.

The easiest part of the entire trip was catching a ride from the airport to Antananarivo. I simply pointed to an address in my Lonely Planet travel guide, threw my bag in the back seat of the taxi and we took off. I was once again stunted by my poor French vocabulary, but I felt confident I'd make due. This was delusion at its best.

We pulled into the gate of the hostel I randomly selected in my book. It looked a little run down, but I had low expectations for ten US dollars a night. And after what I'd just witnessed on the drive, I had absolutely no right to complain about anything – ever again. I walked in with the hopes there was a room available. To my delight the gentleman at the front desk gave me a smile and the universal sign for okay with his thumb and index finger. Before leaving for my room, we managed to coordinate a travel plan using a French/English dictionary, more hand signals and the few French words I remembered. It was my understanding that a taxi would pick me up in the morning and drop me off at a bus station and from there I would leave Antananarivo and head in the direction of Ambalavao, the town closest to the Andringi-tra National Park, with the best hiking in the country. It was Pic Boby, also known as Pic Imarivolanitra, that sealed the deal for booking my flight. It is the highest climbable mountain in Madagascar, with an altitude of 2658 m, and I wanted to see the view from the top.

Morning came and I was all packed and ready to see Madagas-car! I anxiously waited for the taxi to pick me up and daydreamed about the bus ride I was about to experience. How wonderful it was going to be to see the ever-changing landscape – can-yons, mountains, limestone pinnacles, granite peaks, rivers and waterfalls, not to mention pristine beaches, rainforest and tree canopies overrun with lemurs!

The taxi didn't come. I wasn't sure if it was miscommunication or if the driver was just an hour and a half late. I waited patiently in the sun a little longer and eventually a beat-up car clunked through the gate. Better almost two hours late than never. The driver spoke French and quickly realized I was only catching a little bit of what he was saying. I assumed he was apologizing and trying to explain the reason for his tardiness. But I wasn't upset, so I smiled and tried to assure him that everything was okay. With a weak accent, I said, "*Pas de problème*." I wasn't in a huge rush, and every mishap was part of the experience. It was two degrees and rainy at home; waiting in the hot Africa sun was a pretty manageable problem to have.

Back into the chaos of the city streets, we jutted in and out of open spaces on the road, attempting to gain forward momentum toward our destination. If there were no traffic lanes, we'd make one! Women, men and children tapped on the windows of the car asking for money at every opportunity. If the streets were empty, I bet the total drive time to the bus station would have been less than ten minutes, not the 50 minutes it actually took.

When we finally arrived, the taxi driver looked down at my lap and noticed my geeky "bus station" notes that I'd written out in French. I had used my translation dictionary the night before to write out a few sentences to help me communicate where I wanted to go. I anticipated that the station would be total chaos and I didn't want to be an annoying foreigner trying to converse with a little translation book, flipping through pages, wasting time. The sentences "I don't speak French." "Point to the bus to Ambalavao please." "How much?" were written on the page.

The driver took my note, pointed at it and then pointed to himself. He was kindly offering to help me make arrangements! I graciously accepted. We walked into the hysteria of people and weaved toward the disorderly bus lot. The taxi driver yelled over the pandemonium to one of the drivers with what seemed like a question, nodded at the response, then held his hand out to me for bus fare. I handed him some small bills and he passed them over to the driver. I was given a few coins back and permission to step onto the bus. I shook the taxi driver's hand and before he gave it back he kissed it several times. It kind of felt like he was kissing my hand for good luck, like he was a bit worried for me. Ha, I was worried for me too! I had no idea what I was doing or where I was about to go. For all I knew, the bus was going to take me in the opposite direction of where I wanted. I had put all of my faith into a gentleman that showed up two hours late, and to whom I'd only spoken two words.

I stepped inside the bus and sank into a seat. A huge release of stress left my entire body. I had no idea where I was going, how long it would take or what was next when the bus dropped me off. I naively trusted I was going in the direction of Pic Boby and that the remaining details would sort themselves out.

Once about 20 more passengers than seats got settled on the bus, we pulled away. The lady sitting next to me had no choice but to sit partway on my lap since the aisle was full of passengers that were towering overtop of her. Several chickens were in tow and made for an entertaining drive while they clucked over the sound of rickety metal bumping along the highway. The bus made several stops to drop off and pick up passengers en route. It felt like we were going nowhere fast, especially when the bus pulled off the road multiple times for maintenance. The last stop was nearly two hours long and the smoke coming from the hood was an indicator it would be a lot longer. I made a decision to hitchhike to the nearest town and see if I could organize new transportation from there. I saw a few other passengers doing this, so I figured it would be okay for me as well. There were very few vehicles on the highway, so it took a long time before someone approached.

Eventually, a truck pulled to the side of the highway and offered me a ride. I can't explain it, but for some reason I had a bad feeling about the gentleman. He looked friendly enough, but something about his energy didn't sit well with me. I noticed it immediately. I didn't know when the next vehicle would pass by, but I just knew I had to decline his offer. I waved him off and said, "*Merci.*" He screeched back out onto the road in either frustration or anger or both. He had every right to be annoyed with me. But I also had every right to say no.

About 30 minutes later another vehicle approached as I walked down the shoulder of the highway. The sun was hot, but a lovely breeze was making it bearable for an unacclimatized Canadian. "Hello!" an energetic young man yelled out as he waved. *He speaks English!* I was elated. "You need ride?" he asked with a huge infectious smile. "*Merci*! Er, thank you!" I opened the door and awkwardly thanked him in every language I knew. Princi was his name. He looked to be about 20 years old, slightly taller than me at around five feet ten inches, and maybe 100 pounds soaking wet. If he happened to be dangerous, I was fairly confident I could take him.

Luckily, it turned out Princi was a delight! He lived in Antananarivo but was on his way to his village to visit friends and family. With our language barrier I couldn't distinguish whether he was on vacation or had been recently laid off. He worded it, "My boss (Air Madagascar, his employer) gave me a long break." With this information, I wondered if he would be interested in making some extra cash to be my personal driver. I figured it would make the trip so much easier not having to wait for broken buses, and for English translation. When I asked him, he immediately accepted, expressing a lot of excitement. Our plan was to stay a few nights in his coastal village while he spent time with his family and friends, then we'd make our way over to the central part of Madagascar for Pic Boby, then back to the capital city.

The sun was slowly setting as we drove through Princi's village. Small rectangular homes made of clay and grass lined the narrow dirt path we followed. Stick fences surrounded many of the homes to contain the chickens and goats. I had my window down and could feel the warm breeze on my face and the smell of campfire. The light was golden and it accented the hue of the sand and the smooth bark of the baobab trees.

Princi pulled up to the largest building we'd seen in the area and turned the car off. On our drive I had requested to stay at a hostel rather than spend the night with his family. I really wanted the opportunity to spend the night in a traditional Malagasy home, but Princi hadn't seen his family in almost two years. Even with his insistence, it didn't seem right to accept. I'd have the opportunity to see his home and meet his family. I didn't need to spend the entire time with them. "We are here! My friend works at night. You will be safe," Princi assured me. I collected my bag and we walked into the building to discover a lovely young lady behind a desk. She accepted my payment of three US dollars, wrote down my passport information and handed me a towel. We then followed her to a small circular building made of tall wooden rods and what I guessed to be banana leaves on the roof. The sky was pink, but it was light enough to see the soft sand and glorious Indian ocean gently rippling under it. This would be home for the next three nights. My room had a bed inside with a mosquito net around it, and a small sink in the corner that didn't work but looked very pretty. Indoor plumbing wasn't available yet, but they hoped one day it would be. I didn't care at all. This wasn't the accommodation I was expecting – it was better. I had an entire section of seaside to myself!

That evening I slid into the warm sand outside my little hut and read my book with the help of the moon and my headlamp. The water swished back and forth and eventually lulled me to sleep. It wasn't until early the next morning when a few fishermen were preparing for the day that I woke to discover I'd never made it to my room. I sat myself up and surveyed my body for bites – negative – and then went back to sleep in the bed.

A tentative knock on one of the supporting pillars of my quarters woke me back up. I wrapped my towel around me and opened the door to find Princi standing outside. "Happiest Birthday!" he said with a huge smile. "How did you know it was my birthday?" I asked with curiosity and a little delight. "Your passport. My friend noticed," he said with a proud grin. "I will take you on a dhow to snorkel and catch lunch on your special day," he insisted. It was an offer I couldn't refuse. "I will come back in two hours for the trip," he said with excitement in his voice.

I had the perfect opportunity to fit in a workout before we went swimming. I put some clothes on and revisited the soft sand I'd slept on earlier. Initially, I was all alone on the beach performing squats, lunges, push-ups and sprints. But as time went on I noticed a few heads popping up from over the grass fence to observe the crazy white lady next door. I walked over to the fence and looked around it, catching what looked like half the village spying on me! At least two or more dozen men, women and children were watching. I was mortified because of the attention, but also worried that I'd potentially offended someone. The crowd slowly approached me one at a time to shake my hand. I interpreted it as a gesture of acceptance and an opportunity to make me feel welcome. My embarrassment and concern dissolved almost immediately when I felt the warmth and kindness of the local people.

Once I connected with each individual, I walked back to my territory, noticing that several gentlemen were following me. I didn't understand what was going on until one of the fellas started flexing his biceps. *Do they all want to work out?* I wondered. To find out, I pointed to myself and then to them, then flexed and waited to see what kind of response I'd receive. Nothing. Crickets. I stood there like an idiot with my arms up and waited a bit longer, hoping I had not misread the crowd. Relief finally came when they simultaneously nodded in agreement, raised their arms and flexed back. *Well, Happy Birthday to me!* With the language barrier, I just spread my lips as far apart as I could to show how excited I was. They all did the same! *It's on, fellas!*

French was not even an option in this part of Madagascar, so I had to rely on body language and hand gestures entirely. I set up stations that were marked with items of my clothing. Station one was a T-shirt where we did push-ups; station two was a pair of socks where we did burpees (by the way, how many opportunities does a trainer get to demonstrate to a group of adult burpee newbies? So awesome.); station three was marked by my towel where we did walkouts. In total, we had 16 workout stations set up on the beach; one for each of us.

Towering at least five inches over every gentleman in the group, and probably outweighing them by 20 pounds, I looked like a giant pasty-white monster among them. All of the men were in excellent physical condition, likely due to lifestyle – never having "worked out" a day in their lives, because they didn't need to. It became apparent very quickly that many of them had a difficult time with body awareness, making some of their exercise technique a bit iffy. But, hey, they were trying it! There were limbs flying all over the place, torsos snaking in every direction and no appreciation for tempo. But it didn't matter, it was so fun for everyone! We spent the remainder of the morning rotating through all 16 stations not once, not twice, but *seven* times! We were all dead by the end. I had to hand it to the guys; they smiled and laughed the entire time, making the whole experience an absolute pleasure. Nobody took himself seriously; everyone just wanted to try something new, and flex a little (or a lot, in many of their cases). My cheeks hurt almost as much as my body did. As the guys left, they all compared the size of their biceps to one another. It seems no matter what part of the

world I'm in, there is one thing for certain guys have in common:
a desire for big arms.

◎ **I FELT LIKE I HAD TO PINCH MYSELF** a few times to believe
THIS is my life right here, right now! I was perched at the front of a
dhow sailing over crystal clear turquoise water with Princi and
his childhood friend, Fy. Fy was a professional fisherman and
the tallest Malagasy man I had met to date, standing at about
six foot two inches tall. Like the workout crew, he too was about
3 per cent body fat, with smooth skin and a kind, genuine smile.
His gentle nature was immediately noticed; there wasn't an
ounce of judgment in him. In a matter of minutes it felt like I was
a friend, not a foreigner. The sun was hot and directly overhead,
not a cloud in the sky as we bobbed up and down the surface of
the ocean. Fy negotiated the sail like the expert he was and took
Princi and I out to a great snorkelling area. When we arrived, I
leapt off the boat with the snorkel Fy had lent me and scuttled
around the water to the best of my ability. I was taking swimming lessons at the time and was still not very comfortable in
water, but this was not an opportunity I was going to miss out
on because of a healthy dose of fear.

Colourful fish swarmed around me and tickled my bare skin.
Princi encouraged me from the boat: "You are doing good, Anyela!
You are like the fish!" I most certainly wasn't, but it was nice of
him to recognize how difficult it was for me to be in the water. I
was slightly spastic and anything but fluid, but I was making my
way around the boat to see the coral and fish to the best of my
ability. *I could really use a life jacket right about now.* Even with my
nerves, I could appreciate the extraordinary beauty of the sea life
and the warm water. Eventually, I came eye to eye with Fy after
he jumped into the water shortly after me. It took a lot for me
not to instantly latch onto him with all four limbs and use him
as a flotation device. "Be free, Anyela!" Princi yelled out to me,

just when I needed it most. *Yes, be free, Ang. Be cool. You can do this! Water is FUN!* Fy was holding a long spear in one hand and repeatedly diving head first down into the water like he belonged in the ocean. After one dive that felt longer than the rest, Fy reached the surface with a huge lobster on the end of his stick. Princi started cheering and yelled to me, "We have lunch!"

The three of us sat on the beach in the shade and sipped on cola. Fy prepared the lobster and served it up just like Princi said he would. Many of the local villagers stopped by to say hello, which was lovely since some of the faces I recognized from the morning workout. I sat contentedly in the background and listened to the gentlemen banter in their local language. It was a pleasure to be in their company and to feel like I was welcome.

The sun began to slip down into the ocean horizon, creating bronze streaks atop the crests of its ripples. I watched the golden globe intensely, gradually lowering until the last speck of it disappeared. Its light was almost immediately replaced with the candlesticks that were precisely placed on the outside of a birthday cake that two ladies from the village were carefully walking out. The entire group clapped in harmony and cheered. The cake was placed in front of me. It read, "Happy Birthday Angela. 37 Points." I was overwhelmed with the gesture and couldn't even say thank you initially because I was at a loss for words. I blew the candles out and the ladies handed everyone a fork. We all took turns whittling bites off over the course of the evening. Princi later explained to me that every family in the village contributed to purchase the ingredients to have the cake made. The villagers were poor by Western standards – there was no running water, and homes were basic with sand floors – but there was love, community, generosity and happiness like I've never experienced anywhere.

Prior to my time in Princi's village, my birthday was never a big deal for me to celebrate. Since that 37th birthday, where an entire community came together to make the day special for a complete stranger, I've learned that it's important to celebrate one another, because time together is what life is about. We don't know how long we have, so appreciating each day and the milestones matters.

The next morning I packed my bag and met Princi down the road at his family home. I ducked down to fit through the door of the property to meet his mother. She was sitting on a blanket on top of the sand, weaving a grass basket with her twisted, arthritic hands. She looked up at me with peaceful eyes and smiled generously. The room contained one pot filled with water, two other blankets placed on the ground that I suspected to be sleeping areas and a pile of bananas in the corner. Princi's mother gently raised her hand out, indicating she wanted me to approach her. I looked over at Princi for clarification. "She wants to shake your hand," he explained. I walked over, slightly crouched to avoid hitting my head on the roof, and slipped my hand into hers. Her skin was warm and severely weathered, indicative of a long hard life lived. She smiled one more time then kissed the back of my hand. "She wishes you a good journey," Princi said. I took the scarf off the back of my neck and placed it over hers. She looked down at it and stroked it with her disfigured hands in appreciation. "She is very happy. Thank you, Anyela," Princi said with a big smile. "It is time. I will get the wood, then we will go," he said casually, leaving me wondering why wood was so essential.

We slowly rolled along the familiar road we came in on, now exiting the village. I felt saddened to leave but very honoured to have even had the opportunity to stay. If it weren't for the broken bus and meeting Princi, I would have never experienced anything like it. In the midst of my reminiscing, there was a bang on the back of the vehicle that startled us both. Princi put his foot on the brake and paused to see what was happening. A familiar face came out from the back and moved around to my window.

It was Fy! He was out of breath from running to catch up to the vehicle. He hastily handed me two wooden zebu carvings. Princi once again translated for me: "Fy has made you a gift." The zebu is a common animal seen in Madagascar. Basically cattle with humps on their necks, zebu are an important emblem of the country. They symbolize power, strength and prosperity. "Hang these zebu above the doors of your home. The zebu will bring you good wishes and keep you safe," Princi explained. Tears filled my eyes in appreciation as Fy shook my hand and placed his other hand over his heart.

Princi and I drove to the town of Ambalavao where we met another friend of his named Dadou. The two of them had coordinated a meeting over the phone to discuss the logistics of driving to Pic Boby. I didn't know any of the details, but I had the impression the road wasn't in very good condition, and obviously there wouldn't be any signs to point us in the right direction. Dadou lived in the region and offered to join us for the trip to help navigate. I was happy to have him come along, so he hopped into the back seat and we set off.

The drive was spectacular. Winding along the narrow, undulating dirt road past tiered farmland, beautiful clusters of green vegetation and sporadic villages tucked into the landscape. The region had a good supply of water and was clearly fertile, providing the locals with an ample supply of food. We passed over multiple rickety wooden bridges crossing over the river and its many tributaries. Some of the structures were just wide enough to accommodate the tires on our vehicle, and there were no guardrails to protect us. Princi asked Dadou to get out of the vehicle at several bridges to direct him over the wooden planks safely. One slight wrong turn of the wheel and we would go overboard. Dadou would point to the right then left to align our wheels on the bridge, and then give us a forward wave when it was safe to slowly roll toward him.

Rain began to pour down, making the drive slower and very slippery going up hills. Periodically, Dadou would get out of the vehicle and cut branches off nearby trees to lay down in front of us for traction. It was time-consuming but necessary to make any forward progress. Women walked along the side of the road with their beautiful long dresses dragging in the mud while their kids scampered behind in bare feet. Men trudged through the sticky mud with their wooden carts pulled by zebu. Transportation in this region was challenging enough, let alone with harsh rain and muddy conditions. I wondered if anyone ever complained about it. I had a sneaky suspicion not.

◎ **WE ARRIVED AT ANDRINGITRA NATIONAL PARK** where I met my guide, Lobo. I knew from previous African hiking experiences not to assume a certain level of performance based on someone's appearance, but Lobo made this a little more challenging. Standing at approximately four feet five inches tall, and no more than 80 pounds, he was the smallest grown man I'd ever met. He was wearing a full size men's coat that hung down to his knees, accentuating his tiny stature. If it weren't for the beard and hints of grey in his hair, he could have been mistaken for a child, at least from afar. Along with his slight frame came a smugness that was immediately off-putting. He reluctantly shook my hand with limp fingers, making it feel like he wanted as little as possible of his skin to touch mine. I could see it in his eyes; he didn't think I was tough enough to hike the mountain and he thought I had no business being there.

I had decided early on that I wanted to complete the hike in two days rather than the usual three. Everything I had read online was an indicator that the summit was not the grind I yearned for. So when I proposed my plan to increase the daily trekking distance with the intention to make the journey a little more challenging and therefore more appealing, Lobo laughed out loud like I was the most foolish human on Earth. *This feels like Kilimanjaro all over again! Remember your lessons!* I felt very silly and naive arguing with a man who had lived here his entire life. There was a part of me that couldn't help but think his opinion was impacted by a salary cut, but when I offered to pay for three but hike for two, he still wouldn't agree. Obviously, he knew 1,000 per cent more about the hike than I did, so I conceded with his insistence on making it a standard trip in spite of my wishes.

I thought my compromise would have been enough to enable Lobo to respect me just a little, but it was not the case. It was obvious he despised me right from the moment we met, and then my foolish request sent him over the edge. I knew how it looked: a single Western woman strutting into town, wearing her stupid expensive hiking gear, making suggestions on something she really had no knowledge of. In some ways I didn't blame him for resenting me. I was courteous about it, of course, but nonetheless it probably came off as pompous or plain ignorant. With language barriers, cultural differences and previous experiences that have shaped us all, it takes time to understand one another. The great part about hiking is that you are given an opportunity to spend hours with someone to have those discussions and share your perspective. In my opinion it's one of the best ways to learn. I wasn't certain Lobo would be inclined to share in very much conversation, but I was most certainly going to try. *I'm going to defrost this guy! He has no idea what I'm capable of. My goal is to make him smile just once. Oh, and to make the summit.*

Day one of the hike began with an easy walk though the valley. It was a single-track path that weaved through hip-high grass (shoulder height for Lobo) and passed over a creek several times. Initially, there were no trees to grant us relief from the sun, so our pace was a little slower than expected. Lobo was sure to bring it up in order to reinforce the importance of his three-day decision. Once we reached the forest and began to climb a little, our pace improved dramatically. I intentionally crowded Lobo to not so subtly push him faster. He did exactly what I wanted because he was stubborn, just like me. The trees were sparse and fairly short but provided enough relief from the sun's intense rays. "Why did you leave your children?" Lobo asked out of the blue. *Where did that come from? We haven't spoken a word and THIS is the first question he asks me?*

Right away I felt judgment and then I got a little bit defensive. Before I answered, I had to remind myself that I was in an entirely different country with likely very different views; the question was probably quite innocent. "I don't have children," I answered back, with no explanation, trying to keep things simple. "Why don't you have children?" he inquired a little more. I took his questioning a little less offensively and more as an opportunity to share a different perspective with him. "I didn't want to have children," I answered back, very curious about what he'd say next. There was a long pause. "Why?" he finally asked with less judgment and more curiosity. "I'm selfish. I wanted to travel to different parts of the world and hike mountains while I'm young and have my health. That isn't fair to do if you have to leave children at home," I answered honestly. "You like sport?" he asked with shock in his voice. I found it ironic that he'd ask this question while I had clearly travelled a long way to hike a mountain with him. "I do, very much," I replied back. I could see he was trying to fit me inside some kind of box that he understood, but he was having no success. "I like to walk. I like to climb mountains. I like to work. I like to feel my heart beat fast. I like to feel my muscles get sore. I like to be outside," I tried to explain within the limits of our language barrier. "You want to be strong like a man?" he asked with a hint of mockery. "No, I am strong like a lady," I responded back, feeling good about my answer (even though it sounded like a deodorant commercial) but knowing full well he had no idea what that meant.

When we reached the other side of the forest we were presented with a spectacular view of two waterfalls: Riandahy and Riambavy, named after the queen and king. The tale Lobo told was that the king and queen could not conceive until one day they both swam in the pool below the waterfalls. Discounting everything I shared, Lobo insensitively encouraged me to jump in the water so I could "fix" my situation. The coolness would have felt incredible, but there was no way I was touching that water, mostly out of spite, but also just in case the legend were true.

Lobo shook his head appallingly and jumped in with all his clothes on. "I will have many children," he said proudly as he smiled from ear to ear. *You're a very closed-minded little man.* "That is good for you!" I hollered back. I wasn't in the mood to defend my life choices further.

Travelling opens your eyes to just how lucky you are to live in a country where you have options, freedom and the opportunity to be your authentic self. Women in certain areas of Africa have very little choice in who they want to be, or what they want to do. In most cases it is decided from day one that you will be a wife and a mother. Of course, this is wonderful if this is what you want, but if you seek something different, it's very unlikely you'll get it. Lobo had a clear opinion about women and I was messing with his mind. He fluctuated between insulting me (I'm not certain it was always intentional) and curiously seeking more explanation for this perceived obscure life I was leading. With every bit of conversation we had, I could see him slowly opening his mind a little bit more. I didn't expect him to understand or even agree, but signs of decreasing judgment were there.

We arrived at base camp early, which I (of course) pointed out and Lobo ignored. We set up our tents in the grassy area among the roaming zebu. I couldn't believe how many were among us. Their long horns were a little unnerving, especially up close. I expected they would have dispersed in the night, but that was not the case. Instead, they continued to eat the grass around my tent and sporadically let out a sound that made me think of Darth Vader grunting. Between the worry of a zebu walking on my tent and crushing me, and the incredible thunder in the distance, I didn't get a lot of sleep. Our 3:00 a.m. summit departure felt extra early the next day.

It was cold enough to see your breath when we left camp, so Lobo and I both were bundled up in every item of clothing we had. We patiently negotiated the slippery rock beneath us as rain misted our surroundings. The thunder continued to boom and crack in the distance while the sky exploded with light. There were several clouds, but it was fortuitous that there was a perfect opening to enjoy the lightning.

With the help of our headlamps illuminating portions of the trail, we stepped our way up toward the summit of Pic Boby. We steadily climbed for about an hour until Lobo turned to check in on me. "I'm doing great," I responded back enthusiastically, before he could say anything. The truth was I was in my element and loved the quick pace we had going. Lobo was speedy and I was having the best time. He seemed surprised, almost disappointed in my response, so I added a bit of fuel to the fire. "Actually, Lobo, can we go a bit faster? This pace is a little slow for me." I snickered to myself. This was a bit too much fun for me. "Huh" was all he said back, in frustration. *I knew it! He's stubborn like me.* He was still trying to prove his point that we couldn't make it up and down in two days, but his plan was backfiring.

Our hiking pace shifted from brisk to vigorous, which also included some leaping between rocks to keep our rhythm. It felt amazing to feel my heart race, to have to concentrate on the sequence of my breath and to be fully aware of every muscle in my lower half. A few times Lobo turned around to see if he had lost me only to discover I was right there with him. *I'm right here! I'm keeping up just fine, which is so weird since I'm female.* Initially,

I could sense agitation, but it eventually turned to appreciation. *I'm winning you over, Lobo. Be careful, you might have the sudden urge to smile.*

We stood on the summit at an altitude of 2658 metres an hour earlier than planned, which meant we had a while before we could see the sunrise. With all the concentration required to navigate the terrain at the near running pace we held, I didn't notice the rain had ended. Lobo didn't have a waterproof jacket and was soaked through, making the zero-degree temperatures that much colder. I took my coat off and insisted he put it on while we waited to see the sunrise. My experience with Calvin in the Rwenzoris taught me to be persistent under these weather conditions. Lobo refused at first, but luckily the wind changed his mind pretty quickly so we didn't have to argue about it. We sat on the smooth rock and watched the sun slowly make its way up behind the clouds. The sky shifted from a rich golden to a deep pink, highlighted with streaks of orange and blue. Adding to the remarkable landscape was the continued lightning way off in the distance. Lobo and I sat in silence, appreciating that we had the summit and the view all to ourselves.

I took one final deliberate pause to enjoy the moment and feeling one last time. Then, with a big breath, I turned around to chase after Lobo. He wasn't waiting for anything! It was cold and he was over it.

Our descent started off a little slow due to tired legs and stiff knees from the rest period. But, as the sun burned off the clouds, our bodies warmed, consequently increasing our pace. We arrived back at our campsite earlier than Lobo estimated. I, of course, mentioned this with a little pestering wink, and received my *first smile* back! *Is Lobo coming around to me?* I didn't want to push it, so I changed the subject and offered to make some food. "It's my specialty," I bragged. Lobo didn't understand what I was saying. "My best meal," I explained. "Okay, I will have some," he politely accepted, looking a little dubious. I pulled a squished loaf of bread, a jar of peanut butter (from home) and my pocket knife out of my bag and began my ritual. First, I carefully covered every corner of the mangled bread with gooey deliciousness, then gently placed the second slice of bread on top, and placed the delicacy on a flat rock to cut it in half for presentation (obviously), then passed it over to Lobo. "What is this?" he asked, looking very unimpressed. "Try it. You might like it," I said, feeling confident it would speak for itself. He took a very tentative bite and chewed between his front teeth before he committed to pulling it further into his mouth. He paused. Eyebrows rose, causing creases in his forehead as he smiled wide again at me. "VERY GOOD!" he said with enthusiasm. "I like it too!" I said with delight. It was the first time we agreed on something. Once again we sat in silence, this time appreciating the taste of peanut butter, our second natural phenomenon of the day.

When our fancy lunch was complete, I anticipated staying at the camp like Lobo had insisted the day prior. I didn't want to, but he'd shown signs of compromise for me so it was my turn to do the same for him. "Anyela, I think we will go," he said out of nowhere. "Finish today?" I asked, with no jabbing this time. "Yes. I think you are not very tired," he acknowledged. "I would like to continue today. Thank you. I don't think you're tired either," I said respectfully. We proceeded to pack up our camp and finish a day early, just like I'd wanted.

The trip down was glorious. A great deal of focus was necessary to prevent tripping and falling, but we managed well. Leaping and bounding between rocks, scampering down sections of scree and soil, and jogging flatter terrain when we could made it feel like we were in an adventure race.

We eventually arrived at the "fertility pond," as I called it, where Lobo and I shared another peanut butter sandwich (at his request). Our comfortable silence was broken when Lobo looked up at me and said, "You are a very different girl." I wasn't sure if it was a compliment or a complaint so I didn't respond, hoping he'd explain what he meant. Unfortunately, he didn't. We finished our sandwiches and freely jogged through the deep fields of grass toward our starting place. The sun was hot, the air was clean and my body felt weightless as my feet effortlessly bounded forward. When I'm feeling stressed and need to find a happy place, this memory is where I go. The dentist has never been so pleasant since Madagascar!

Sweat dripped down my forehead as Lobo and I coasted in under the large trees surrounding the national park entrance. We were a day early, so I'd have to wait for the boys to travel back to get me with the vehicle. Lobo made the call and informed me that it wouldn't be very long. They were camping just a few kilometres down the road from where we were. We sat in silence together one final time until Lobo spoke. "You are very different." I was surprised he was bringing it up again. I patiently waited for an expansion of his thought this time around. Nothing. *Dude! Is there something you're trying to tell me? I've got feelings, you know. Spit it out!*

I pondered his silence while we waited. *Was this a language barrier issue, or a criticism he felt required no further explanation, or simply a...* "It is good," he suddenly said. This time there was more. "You love sport. I see it with my eyes. You are happy." I was about to respond when he continued, "You are strong in your heart and in your body." I smiled at him with appreciation. It felt really nice to be seen and to hear him acknowledge it. I knew I confused the hell out of him in the beginning, but he somehow was starting to get it. I'm pretty sure he still would not fully agree with my life choices, but it was impressive that he was able to respect them despite their being so unorthodox for the world he knew. "You taught me," he smiled with a little shake of his head in disbelief. "A lady with no children – it is okay. I see. You. Are. Happy. Never would I have believed this before." I nodded my head humbly and thanked him for being open to listening. He paused for a moment then lightened the mood with, "And you showed me Peeaannuutt Buutterr! I learned a lot."

The boys rolled up as the clouds closed in like curtains on a window. I passed my coat over to Lobo as a parting gift and he graciously accepted it. "There's a surprise in there for you," I said with anticipation. He opened the coat up to discover the remainder of the peanut butter. He smiled wide. "I love it! Thank you very much. This will make me very strong. Next time, it will only be one day to Pic Boby!"

We took the same road back out from Pic Boby toward the highway. I was delighted to have the chance to enjoy the journey one more time. The valleys of terraced farmland surrounded by thick forest were enough to keep me engaged for hours. It turned out to be market day as well, which provided extra interest to the drive. Observing what locals were transporting, appreciating the vibrant dresses the ladies were wearing and witnessing daily life in rural Madagascar was a real treat. Very few people wore footwear, and most walked many kilometres to the market every week. There were a few bicycles on the road, but the rutty terrain didn't make it easy to ride them. Instead, most were used as transporters for large quantities of produce or small animals as the owners walked alongside them.

There were very few motor vehicles of any kind on the road. Princi suggested it was because the locals couldn't afford them, and the road conditions would make it impossible to accommodate traffic of any kind anyway. The only other vehicles we came across were large trucks transporting mostly rice to the markets. As we bumped along the dusty road, Dadou pointed to one of the large trucks parked in the centre of a hectic market. The back half of the truck was filled with a huge mound of rice, as two men were scooping it into satchels and passing them down to local customers. But it wasn't the rice Dadou was interested in; it was the stack of wooden planks tucked inside the truck. I thought nothing of it initially until it jogged my memory of the wood Princi collected before we left his village. It wasn't firewood; these were boards similar to what you'd use to build a fence. Dadou was noticeably irritated. His volume of speech increased as he went though a long-winded rant in Malagasy that started off frustrated and ended angry.

I was sitting in the back this trip and I could see Princi's eyes look up at me in the rear-view mirror. "Why is that wood so special Princi?" I asked him. "There are very big problems here. I hoped it would not be, but it is," he started to explain. "Problems? What do you mean?" I asked with curiosity and unnatural excitement. The vehicle pulled to a stop and, without having to say a word, Princi directed my eyes to the bridge in front of us, which had been stripped of 50 per cent of its wooden planks. "The big trucks, they steal the wood from the bridges," Princi explained. "What! Why?" I asked with shock. "So nobody else can sell rice at the market," he replied, shaking his head.

My naive mind couldn't believe it. *How could anyone be so selfish that they would literally tear the wood off a bridge platform to prevent anyone else from crossing?* The piles of planks Dadou spotted inside the transport truck were stored so they could lay them back down when they were ready to cross back over and drive to the capital city. It was obvious this was known information because Princi packed wooden planks in anticipation of this.

Dadou and Princi jumped out of the vehicle and carried several boards to the bridge. We didn't have enough of them to fill all of the gaps (we would have needed at least 40 or 50, instead of the seven we had), so they covered the hole closest to us, then Princi drove far enough ahead to collect the loose planks we'd just driven over. Dadou passed the planks to me one by one through the window and then carefully sidestepped along the vehicle, collecting one plank at a time to place them in the next bridge gap ahead of us.

The entire process was terrifying. The bridge was barely wide enough for the vehicle in the first place, let alone to allow Dadou to shuffle back and forth from my window to the front with a long wooden plank in tow. It was daunting to precariously sit idle on a rickety bridge overhanging the surging river three stories below us. When Princi was ready to drive the vehicle over the newly laid planks in front of us, I was instructed to open my door so Dadou had something to hang onto. The boards weren't nailed back on, so they slipped a little under the wheels as we rocked over them. It was unnerving every time we could feel the vehicle spit a plank out from behind its wheels. When the door was open, I could see down between the plank gaps, realizing just how high up we were and how tenuous the platform really was. All three of us would take a pause in relief after we'd successfully crossed the bridge. My mind couldn't help but recount just how many more we crossed on the way in. I very naively suggested that just one bridge down would be enough to keep most vehicles away, but that didn't stop the drivers from dismantling every structure anyway. With every crossing we approached, it became apparent this would be a long, scary trip home.

Each bridge varied in length, but every single one had at least a third, if not more, of its boards confiscated. It took at least an hour to cross some of the longer ones. Meanwhile, locals were still trying to navigate their way to the market, so accommodating zebu, goats and hundreds of people added another chaotic element to an already nerve-racking situation. Some of the locals carried a single board along with them, placing it inside a large gap to shorten their step. They would pick it up from behind them, and then place it in another large hole. It was a similar process to what we were doing, just on a smaller scale. It was clear they were used to this routine, unfazed and determined to make it to the market regardless of the tremendous inconvenience and danger.

At one point Princi got hung up on one of the bridges, but we didn't have enough planks to cover the next hole so he could press on the gas pedal in order to propel out of it. He yelled at me to get out of the vehicle and carefully walk off the bridge. He didn't say it, but I knew he was fearful of the vehicle tipping over the side and he didn't want me in it. I gingerly stepped out onto the loose planks below my door. It appeared to be equal distance to either side of the crossing, so I figured I might as well go forward not back. Dadou walked alongside me as the muddy water crashed against the rocks below us, making it much more difficult to focus. "More adventure," he said with a little terror in his voice but attempting to make me feel okay. I laughed, as I do when I'm nervous or uncomfortable. Dadou began to laugh too, which caused me to laugh more and more until we were hysterical, straddled as far as my legs would go between boards and frozen together holding hands. I had tears running down my face and I became almost as fearful of peeing myself as I was of falling into the opening between our legs. "Hey! No time for laughs," Princi yelled out over the commotion while Michael Bolton's "How Can We Be Lovers" blared unexpectedly out of his speakers. Meanwhile, a herd of zebu and several locals stopped in front of us, equally perplexed by the large hurdle and perhaps more so by the loud music, causing my laughter to flare up again in response to the absurdity of the situation. *What the actual hell is going on here? What random world am I living in?*

Almost as if it were a response to my internal questions, a large Darth Vader growl came from one of the zebu causing me to officially lose it. My laughter was out of control, and my legs were spread too far apart to prevent it, even with my last resort bend at the waist. My fear became a reality. I peed my pants!

Of course, it wasn't quick either. It was of the Tom Hanks-*A League of Their Own* variety. *Oh my word! Why do I have to pee so much? I can't make it stop! This is my nightmare!* "It is okay, Anyela. Everyone has done this," Dadou said with absolutely zero concern or judgment in his voice. "It is natural. Be free," he added nonchalantly. It felt very strange to converse with him openly while peeing my pants on a bridge, but I did. "You are very kind, Dadou. Thank you for that." What? What was I supposed to say to him? Do you have a better response?

When the longest pee of my life was over, I was quickly jolted back to the larger calamity at hand: straddling two wooden planks over an angry river. While holding hands, Dadou and I were able to push off our back feet and successfully leverage onto the other side of the gap. Thanks to the generosity of the locals, we were successful in crossing the bridge with the use of their extra loose boards. A crowd of kids surrounded me, touching me gently on the hands and staring. It was uncomfortable to be the centre of attention, but a great distraction from my pant-wetting embarrassment. The little girls picked at the small hairs on my arms in fascination, while the little boys pulled at my hands, encouraging me to play. I looked over at the vehicle stopped midway on the bridge, surrounded by zebu and locals trying to squish past. Princi poked his head out his window, attempting to drive forward with Dadou's direction. I was astonished at what I was witnessing, but even more mind-boggled when I realized I was the only one watching! The freckles on my shoulders were apparently more exciting than the craziness on the bridge.

As soon as the crowd of chaos cleared and it was "safe," I joined back in to help transport the wooden planks. Dadou stood at the back of the vehicle and I was at the front. He collected the boards and passed them one at a time to me so I could place them down on the bridge to fill the holes. Princi continued to drive forward, just one to two feet at a time until we finally made it to the other side.

Once it was all over the three of us had a group hug in celebration and relief. *Man, I wouldn't want to hug me right now!* There was just one desire that needed to be met before we turned onto the highway for the long drive to the capital: a shower. Of course, I knew this wasn't an option, but I was desperate, so I asked if I could walk down to the river to clean up. They agreed very quickly to this idea, proving just how bad I must have smelled.

I quickly walked down to the water by myself and undressed cautiously, looking for peering eyes. Once I felt the coast was clear, I stepped into the brown water to rinse myself off. It was cold and filthy and I pondered what disease I might catch as I washed my bits. I would be sure to not tell my friends at Atlas Immunization (the travel health clinic) about this; they would not be impressed! As I stood naked in the water, a large group of people showed up out of nowhere. *Yes, of course. How could I have ever thought this would go smoothly?* There I was, with at least five families' worth of people, several zebu, of course, and a couple of goats perched on the riverbank gawking at me as if I were an extraterrestrial. Paranoia about parasites shifted to offending anyone in the community. *Am I allowed to bathe in this river? I hope I'm not disrespecting anyone. Princi wouldn't lead me astray. Although...I was smelly.* I don't know how long I stood wondering, but it was long enough to see that several naked people were coming in to join me. *Whew!* I've never been more relieved to swim in dirty river water with naked strangers and humpbacked cows. Paranoia crept back in once again as I contemplated how I would walk out of the water to put my clothes on without anyone noticing.

My solution to the predicament may not have been my best. Funny, at the time it seemed so good in my head, though. I crouched down into the smallest version of myself, rounded my back and waddled like a penguin toward my shorts. This was my attempt to keep things discreet. In the end, I just looked like Gollum in *The Hobbit*. I blame one of the zebu for hijacking

176 ☒ BE FREE

my plan by standing firmly on my clothes. My *Crouching Tiger, Hidden Dragon* position was not ideal for zebu negotiating, so I ended up having to stand, bare all and prod him forward off my shorts. Naturally, he didn't want to cooperate so a very helpful gathering of children ran over to assist naked me. The zebu eventually got the hint, but not before he went number two all over my shorts. *NO! NO! NO! That did NOT just happen!* My clothes were no longer an option, and I had no other choices. So, yeah, I had to walk naked back to the car to find something else to wear. *Ha! And I thought peeing my pants would be the most embarrassing part of my day!* Princi and Dadou saw me coming and respectfully turned around. "A zebu shit on my clothes, guys. I'm really sorry you have to see this," I said, absolutely mortified. "It is okay, Anyela. Be free," Princi said just as kindly as Dadou had earlier. *Be free. I think that's good advice. But I think I still need some pants.*

All three of us hopped inside the vehicle, rolled down our windows to let the breeze in and set off for the highway like nothing strange had occurred all day. Princi turned up the volume on his stereo when the cassette tape made its way back around to Micheal Bolton. Together, at the top of our lungs, we sang along to "How Can We Be Lovers."

KENYA

Approximately 9:00 a.m.

THE HIKE DOWN was slow and steady. Our original plan was to make it a two-day journey, but Samuel's limp was not improving and it was evident he needed to get home and recover as soon as possible. We decided to walk all day in order to arrive at Samuel's village by mid-afternoon. The trail was slippery and cluttered with roots and rocks, making every awkward step very painful for his swollen ankle. Our pace was incredibly slow and I wondered if our decision was the better of the two options. The sun was in our favour most of the morning, but around 1:00 p.m. familiar clouds rolled in and pounded us with rain again. It made the red clay path slick and challenging to navigate for the last few hours. Samuel's foot was sliding out the front of his boot, causing him to wince in agony every time due to the extra movement it caused in his lower leg.

We took a short break and sat underneath a canopy of trees to have a snack and relieve Samuel of some of his suffering, even if temporarily. I could tell we were getting close to the main gate based on the terrain we were following. The narrow mountain trail had transitioned to a wide rutty road that had potholes in some places nearly knee deep. There was a loud tractor slowly grinding up the slick, uneven road toward us.

While the driver rolled his green machine aggressively over the mounds of the slippery red earth beneath it, he caught a glimpse of us sitting in the trees. He made his way out of a deep crater and stalled on a relatively flat surface, then turned the massive tractor off, stepped down, and down and down again, and jogged toward us. It seemed (to me) that he was speaking very fast and frantically to Samuel. The two of them conversed in Swahili for a few minutes as I tried to read their faces and formulate an idea of what the topic of conversation was. I guessed it had something to do with the weather conditions based on Samuel's hand gestures indicating (what I thought was) the amount of snow we had walked through. The tractor driver looked very concerned and upset as he spoke to Samuel. Every once in a while they would both look over at me at the same time. I wasn't sure if it was their way of trying to include me, or if they were talking about me and were checking in to see if I was picking up on what they were saying. The conversation abruptly ended and the gentleman ran back to his tractor.

"Do you want to know something?" Samuel asked cryptically. "It is very bad." I had no clue what he was about to tell me, and I wasn't sure I wanted to know. "How bad is it?" I asked with concern. "The man we saw before the summit. You remember?" he asked with a different look of pain on his face than the one for his ankle. "The British gentleman in the yellow pants?" I confirmed. "Yes, that man." Samuel took a long pause. "He lost sight of his guide in the snow. They got split apart." I processed the information and then asked, "Is the tractor man going to rescue him?" There was another long pause from Samuel that felt like an eternity. "It is still snowing. Rangers looked all night and today they looked with his guide...but he is nowhere."

Tears filled both our eyes. I couldn't help but remember how happy the gentleman was to have summited. He couldn't wait to share the news with his family. "Do you think they will find him?" I asked with a small amount of hope in my voice. "No. The snow is very bad and the rangers cannot see anything." Samuel explained to me that the gentleman's guide believed his client had accidently walked off the cliff due to the poor visibility. I closed my eyes and tears turned to sobbing. I was transported back to where we had met him. It would have been so easy to take one wrong step and fall victim to the mountain. I composed myself and turned to Samuel to say, "Thank you. Thank you for insisting we sit by that rock for as long as we did. Thank you for your patience. Thank you for getting us down safely." "It is my job, Anyela," he said with modesty. "I know it is, but sometimes you can't outsmart the mountain and terrible things happen," I replied back. "This is why it is an adventure. You cannot predict," he spoke wholeheartedly. "I'm very grateful I was with you," I said while patting him on the knee. "I was scared too, Anyela. Your stories helped me. Thank you," he kindly replied back. We sat in silence for a few moments to reflect on and appreciate what we had. Before we stood up to continue down to the gate, I had to point out the obvious, just to get it off my mind. "Samuel, that could have been us." He looked over at me and replied with sincerity in his eyes, "Yes. But it was not God's wish."

The rest period we took didn't seem to help Samuel's ankle one bit. His limp was hard to watch, yet out of concern I couldn't take my eyes off of him. In an attempt to distract him, I asked, "Samuel, do you want to hear my final story?" He stopped in place and turned to look at me. "Yes. It would be a pleasure."

THE CONGO

"WHY ON EARTH would you want to go there?" was the question I was asked by every single person upon disclosure of my next travel destination. The Democratic Republic of Congo (DRC), also known as the Congo. The country was under a severe travel advisory (and still is today) due to the instability of the country. The Government of Canada had issued an "Avoid All Travel" warning on its website. I was familiar with the "Avoid All Necessary Travel" advisory I'd seen so many times, but this was on a whole new level. It meant that if assistance were required while travelling through the country, it would likely not be provided due to the high risks associated for the aid workers.

The DRC at the time was listed as one of the top ten most dangerous places on Earth. It was definitely not a typical vacation getaway, and it was certainly unfortunate that Mount Nyiragongo (a rare, hikeable, active volcano, with the largest, most accessible lava lake on Earth; aka, catnip for adventure seekers) was located on the eastern side of the country, in the heart of the area most impacted by the rebels and the ongoing civil war. Rape, gun violence, kidnapping and even Ebola were serious concerns. I was foolish (that's being kind) to even think of the idea, let alone book a flight to Africa with full intentions of hiking the volcano to see the seductive cauldron of lava at the top with my own eyes. At the time, flying directly into the Congo was expensive, inconvenient with so few flight options and involved lengthier inland travel to Mount Nyiragongo, increasing the risk of running into the wrong people, at the wrong time. I figured the less time I spent in the country the better, so I opted to fly to Rwanda instead. The plan was to cross the border into the city of Goma on foot. It would then only require a 15-kilometre drive inland to reach the base of Nyiragongo. This proactive decision made me feel more confident about the journey, but I wasn't convincing anyone else that my short three-day visit would be worth it. I wasn't fully convinced either, but my compulsion to satisfy my curiosity overshadowed the risks.

I'm not proud of this, but it's the truth. Once I get an idea in my head, I can't shake it! How many opportunities do we get in our lives to hike to the top of a volcano and look down into a crater of bubbling lava? That sounds like something you only see in the movies. These were the stories I told myself for years. I knew there was tremendous uncertainty in going, but I had my mind made up.

So there I was, alone in Kigali, Rwanda, with no cell phone and no solidified plans. I sat in the airport with my backpack by my feet where I crouched down to sit and put my head over my knees to mentally prepare. I took a few deep breaths, focused on the present moment and embraced the discomfort of my nervous energy. I was ready to do this! I knew what I wanted; I just needed some help with how to make it happen. I took a cab to the centre of town and rested my head for the night at a cheap hotel. The next day I met a local gentleman in the tiny hotel lobby who introduced me to a cousin of his who had guiding experience. I explained my intention to hike Mount Nyiragongo and asked for assistance to drive me to the border and potentially help negotiate my visa entry. I had read about the corruption of the Congolese government and was informed that it trickled down to the police force and border patrol officers in some cases. I didn't know how accurate the information I had was, but I figured having local backup was a good idea, in case the harassment claims at the border were indeed as bad as they sounded.

Edward, my guide, had only been to the border of Rwanda and Congo once in his lifetime, and that was several years prior. He spoke about it like a tourist would – almost boasting that he'd been. He was excited to make the trip with me, but he was clearly inexperienced and needed some current advice on how to attain a visa, and preferably without paying an atrocious fee for it. Before our departure we sat on the side of the road for about an hour while Edward made a few phone calls to eventually connect with another gentleman who lived directly in Goma, Congo. Julian was his name, and he was the cousin of a friend of a sister's friend. So, obviously, we could totally trust him. He was basically a family member! Every once in a while Edward would translate back to me what the two of them were discussing. He informed me that I would indeed have to walk across the border like I had read online. A vehicle with Rwandan licence plates was at risk of vandalism if driven into the Congo. There was still a great deal of animosity between the Congo and Rwanda since the 1994 genocide. It was arranged over the telephone that the local Goma gentleman would handle my visa purchase at the border crossing. Edward would drive me to the gate and I would be handed off to Julian. We were told the process would take some negotiating but were assured our journey there would not be wasted.

This was a window of opportunity when the conflict had been in a lull and visas were being granted to dumb tourists such as myself. I would get in. How much it would cost me was unknown and my suspicions were that the fee would be a bit higher to line Julian's pocket. Everything about the plan seemed shady and full of uncertainty. But, honestly, what else would have I expected? I was going to the Congo, not Disneyland!

Hours of scenic mountain views and clusters of smiling people walking in colourful garments to and from the market kept me in wonder and awe with every twist and turn in the road. We eventually laid eyes on Lake Kivu in the distance and followed the highway down to the beautiful blue water surrounded by lush green vegetation. This was the lake that Mount Nyiragongo's lava flowed into after the 2002 eruption. It was that lava that formed the peninsula supporting a portion of Goma city upon which it was rebuilt. Edward pointed it out to me, to our left. This was the indicator that we were only minutes away from the border. I could feel my heartbeat in my throat as Edward straightened up, rolled his window down and removed his sunglasses for the armed officers that slowly approached the vehicle.

The four officers spoke in French and asked Edward to get out of the truck. My French was limited, so I only caught a little bit of what they were asking. I was relying on body language to determine if this was a positive or negative interaction. All of a sudden I heard a fist pounding on my window. A fifth officer came from behind the vehicle and asked me to get out too. I felt so vulnerable with absolutely zero chance of defending myself verbally or physically if I needed to. I had to trust that everything was fine. We had nothing to hide, so I stood as casually as I could as the men took everything out of the truck to inspect it. Minutes later Edward was given the nod of approval to continue forward to the gate on foot. *That's it?* That went way better than I expected it to. Then one of the officers unnecessarily helped me put my backpack on and gave me an unappealing, amorous grin while he tucked some of my hair behind my ear. *And it's time to walk away from this creep. Walk fast. But in a cool, collected way. Don't freak out! Don't let him see your fear. Be cool. And under no circumstances do you look back. Pretend he's not there watching you. Stop swinging your arms so much. Act natural. Na-tur-al. You've got this.* My mind was running away from me and I was trying to reel it in so it wouldn't translate outwardly.

Edward was still collecting his items and tossing them back into the truck when I reached the border gate. Under normal circumstances I would have stayed to help him. This was not one of those average days. I had lost all politeness and was in freak-out-inside, cool-outside balancing mode! There were nearly a dozen armed men mingling around the premises. I could only imagine what they were thinking when they saw me walk up the road. Among the military guards, behind the metal gate, was a stout man in blue trousers with a dusty white dress shirt buttoned down to reveal a chest of gold chains. It was Julian, our local bureaucratic fixer. I don't like to make judgments on appearance alone, but sometimes when you're travelling by yourself you do. My initial thoughts? *Oh boy, this visa process is going to be something to watch. This guy looks like a grinder, but he'll get me in for sure. I'm just going to have to pay attention to the transaction details, because I'm not sure he can be fully trusted.*

Edward eventually joined the two of us and we sat down on the concrete step to discuss the process. Julian would require some money upfront, along with my passport, a completed visa request form, my yellow fever card,[1] and a letter of invitation that Julian had written in advance.

The visa negotiation process felt similar to buying a car. Julian would present me with a fee for the visa that was five times more than what it actually cost, so I'd refuse. He would walk back to the visa counter and chit-chat with the officer for a few minutes then return back with a new fee that was slightly lower but

---

1 A very valuable piece of paper, a yellow fever card proves you have been vaccinated for yellow fever within the last ten years. Without a yellow fever card, there are many countries you cannot enter, even with a passport. These cards are not easily attainable in Africa and are a hot commodity. This is why they are a popular item to steal and why it's important to keep your eyes on yours at all times.

still ridiculous. The back and forth routine occurred four times until we settled on double what the visa was actually supposed to cost, according to the information I had read online. As shady as I thought Julian was, I truly don't think I would have been granted a visa without him that day. After about two hours of negotiation, my passport was officially stamped for entry. Unfortunately, we were still not in the clear. I realized my yellow fever card was missing. The visa officers insisted they gave it to Julian, but I trusted him more than them. Eventually, after continually annoying them with broken French questions, one of the officers handed the card over to me reluctantly. I was actually surprised they didn't make me pay for it.

There were three other tourists from Israel waiting on the steps of the border patrol building who were denied access after waiting several hours. This had been their second attempt to obtain visas over the course of a few weeks. Having a local vouch for you appeared to be effective. I was in. *Holy shit, I'm in!*

Once I was officially granted access, I said goodbye to Edward as I hopped into a different truck with Julian and two police officers who escorted me to a hostel just on the outskirts of town. I barely knew Edward, but somehow having him by my side gave me a little comfort. As the truck pulled away from him at the border, I instantaneously felt very alone. I had to trust that slick Julian would have my best interests at heart, not just his.

Within minutes, the road transitioned abruptly from a smooth paved surface to rutted pavement laden with trash and rubble. The lush green vegetation backdrop was replaced with dilapidated concrete buildings surrounded by security walls that had shards of glass embedded on the tops of them. Men and women covered their faces as they walked the streets in an effort to keep the debris out of their lungs and eyes. Children were covered in dust and threadbare clothes and there were no smiles. White UN trucks, OXFAM vehicles and huge green tanks on nearly every

corner jolted me with a dose of reality. This devastating environment was the consequence of a volcanic eruption and an ongoing
war. It literally felt like we had driven from heaven straight into
hell. As we made our way to the hostel I was sternly told that
under no circumstance was I to walk outside without an escort –
day or night. Not even to cross the street.

The truck took a left turn into a poorly gated complex. If
anyone wanted access to the buildings, it would take almost
no effort to kick down the fence. I guess that's why they had
two armed guards on either side giving us the okay nod to pass
through. Inside, there was an open grassy area in front of several small buildings that appeared to be a relaxation place for
several UN members. They were drinking beer, smoking cigarettes and catching some rays. I felt like Forrest Gump when he
first flew to Vietnam and met Lieutenant Dan on his first day
in camp. Once again I had to pull up my confident pants, get
out of the truck and act like nobody would notice. *They're not
watching, nobody cares! You're blending in just fine.* I walked along
with my head down a bit to avoid eye contact with the men as
Julian escorted me to the hostel entrance. I tried to ignore the
whistling, hooting and hollering. "Do you know them?" Julian
asked, obliviously. I laughed and said no. He then suggested that
it would be a good time to have a drink with them. "It probably
would be, Julian. But I'm going to get some rest today." Then I
gave myself a little internal praise. *See, you're not a total idiot! You
make some good decisions.*

It turns out that hostel is still one of the scariest places I've
ever slept in my life. Even the dozen or so UN members living
there didn't make it feel safe. There were holes in the walls of my
room that made me feel like I'd be watched at some point during
my stay. Several holes led to outside and two large holes led to
the room next to me. The gentlemen in one of the rooms next
door were clearly intoxicated and periodically challenged each

other to wrestling matches. As the night went on, their level of intoxication increased, as did the laughter and what sounded like damage to the room. It was unnerving to know that the wall between us was so thin it could literally be kicked in.

The sun had set hours ago and I had spent the later part of the day reading while nestled in the crevasse of the warped mattress that nearly touched the floor. It was almost a hammock, not a bed at this stage of its life.

It was time to sleep, but I couldn't help listening for warnings that someone was going to enter my room, either by walking in or being aggressively shoved through the wall. The party next door didn't seem to be ending anytime soon.

I wanted to go for a run so badly – to get away from the chaos and to release some stress. I highly doubted Julian was interested in escorting me for such an activity at this hour (or any hour). It may come as a surprise, but I picked up on the fact that it probably wasn't a good idea to go out alone. Instead, I planned out a HIIT (high intensity interval training) workout that I did in the little space beside the bed. The workout had the desired effect of relieving some nervous energy and taking my mind off my uncomfortable surroundings. Ironically, all of the jumping, huffing and puffing resulted in one of the drunken fellas next door knocking on the wall to see if I was okay. I had my headphones on and didn't realize I was making more noise than they were at one point! A couple more guys from the communal grassy area knocked on my door to see if I needed assistance also. I explained what was going on and they laughed with relief. These guys are cool, I thought. The interaction was probably one of the best things that could have happened. The noise level didn't improve, but knowing that someone was looking out for me put my mind at ease and allowed me to consider getting some shut-eye.

In preparation for that, I pulled the sheet back on the mattress to discover bed bug debris in the creases, so I opted to sleep on the wooden floor with my sleeping bag instead. It was a warm evening, but I insisted on keeping my sleeping bag zipped to the top with the hood over my head to help prevent the cockroaches from crawling in. It wasn't the most glamorous time in my life, but I kept reminding myself that it would all be worth it. This trek was going to be epic! I put one earbud in and listened to slow, calming music (it was Yanni; don't judge me) and left the other ear available to listen for intruders of the insect and/or human variety, just in case.

The next day I woke up from a surprisingly great sleep. It was still dark outside and I was a bit scared to turn my headlamp on to find crawly critters on me. As soon as the light went out the previous evening I could hear them scuttling across the wooden planks. My hand frantically searched around the inside of my sleeping bag for the lamp so I could do some inspecting. Before I turned it on, I made a deal with myself. *Five critters or less will indicate a fantastic day. Okay, maybe ten or less. But if there are 50 critters, I go back to Canada. Well, maybe no more than 40. Actually, no more than 33 critters (all of which must be less than the size of a loonie) and that's my final deal. Okay, go ahead and see the damage. Please let there be ten or less. Please, please, please.*

I poked my headlamp out the hole of my sleeping bag where my face was and switched it on to discover that no intruders of any kind had nestled on top of me! Rock on! Today is going to be a great day. *Whoohoo! Here I come Nyiragongo!* Then I looked next to me, under the caved-in bed, and witnessed a small gathering of auburn-shelled crustaceans minding their own business. There were definitely more than ten, but I wasn't going to count since they weren't on me. I felt like that was fair deal.

◎ **"WHAT DO YOU MEAN SHOT?"** I asked with grave concern. Over two hard-boiled eggs at breakfast, Julian shared the news that two park rangers had been killed around Mount Nyiragongo the afternoon prior. It was suspected that the M23 rebels were responsible. The information was scary enough on its own, but then to hear the number of people that would be escorting me up the volcano was an indicator that the shooting was not a one-off – this could easily happen again. We would have two military with us in the truck for the 15-kilometre drive to the base of Nyiragongo, two park rangers and one guide. Julian asked me if I wanted to carry a machete and I laughed, remembering my time in the Bwindi Impenetrable Forest in Uganda, having to hack my way through to see the gorillas. "Is there a lot of vegetation to cut through?" He looked at me like this was a silly question. "No, it's for protection." When he saw I was aghast, he backpedalled with a laugh suggesting he was making some incredible joke. I went along with it, but I knew he wasn't kidding. *A machete? What am I getting myself into here? Even Julian sounds a little freaked out. Remember, zero roaches were on you. That was the deal. It's going to be all right.* I know; it's insane I was using that as my litmus test for security. Let's not dwell on it, and move on. Anyway...

The UN fellas played hard, but they also worked hard. The entire complex had been cleared out and all their vehicles had fled for duty. I organized my backpack, then Julian and I set off with the military escorts for one of the most enlightening 15 kilometres of driving I've ever experienced.

UN bases were set up all along the road leading to Nyiragongo. Julian pointed them out by country as we approached each one. "There is UN Italy, UN Congo, UN China..." It was just one base after another. There were so many brave people in the Congo doing their best to acquire peace for the country. Huge fences, old warplanes and military towers lined the dusty road we bumped along. The troops were intended to make you feel safe, but their enormous presence brought attention to just how dangerous the circumstances really were. Large trucks filled with 100 or more men and women passed us as they made their way to the next city for work. Shoeless women and children navigated over large piles of volcanic rocks that were still covering a large percentage of the land since the eruption in 2002. A significant part of the area had been covered at one time and it was now nearly a decade later and the devastation was still very evident. Children as young as 2 years old carried rocks for their mothers to help clear land around their thatched-roof homes.

There were so many resources needed, but the war didn't make it easy or safe for aid workers to stay long. The Congo is so rich in culture and could be a mecca for tourism, but the instability of the country is very worrisome. I was pleased to be supporting local guides and park rangers instead of hiring a large foreign travel organization, but I also felt guilty putting anyone in danger. Every kilometre we gained felt just a bit less safe as we headed further east. I hoped that if we were in serious danger someone would have said something. But I'm not certain they would have. I think sometimes perspectives can become skewed and survival instincts can mask reality.

We arrived at the base of Mount Nyiragongo where I met the park rangers (Damien and Peter), and my hiking guide (Henry), who would be escorting me up to the crater rim. The mood was solemn. Henry explained to me that nearly 130 of his colleagues had been killed in the past ten years. The news of the two gentlemen joining the list yesterday was still fresh and understandably emotional. He kindly tried to change the subject and ensure me that we would be safe. He asked if I wanted to carry a machete, for comfort's sake. This time I considered it for a moment and then declined. Never did I imagine I'd be asked that question for that reason twice in my life, let alone in the same day. If the AK-47s the fellas were carrying weren't going to be enough, a machete certainly wasn't going to save me. (Especially if I was using it, since I have a hard enough time cutting vegetables.)

We began the hike with a photo next to the original entrance sign, "Parc National Albert," which was the park name before it became Virunga National Park. It was peppered with bullet holes, which inappropriately made me laugh. I had to put it in my mind that it was simply used as target practice for bored park rangers. *What am I doing here? Well, you're here now. All these people have made huge efforts to help you. Now is not the time to change your mind. Besides, you've been informed that if there were a serious risk, the park would be closed to tourists. Oh, and zero cockroaches.*

The hike began around 2000 metres and was a steady climb. There were narrow switchbacks carved between the lava rocks. Henry explained that our hiking direction was following the path the lava took during the 2002 eruption. The lava hardened and created a black rocky terrain that wobbled under our shoes. At the time of the eruption, the lava did not come out from the top of the volcano like you'd see in cartoons. It seeped out of the fissures lower down and slowly moved toward Goma, destroying about 15 per cent of the city, forcing the evacuation of 400,000 people and making tens of thousands of people homeless.

It was a sunny, hot day as we consistently stepped upward for about three and a half hours. The steep sections felt great on the legs! Clouds began to roll in as we approached the top at 3470 m. My first view of the summit was the seven-kilometre diameter rim releasing steam from the hot lava below. It was billowing out quickly and shifting with the wind as it picked up. Henry seemed disappointed with our view and was apologizing for it, but I was elated. I was grateful just to be in Africa, on top of an active volcano, with three great companions.

Once the sun went down, the four of us bundled up and sat in a circle together chatting over soup and pasta. It was a wonderful way to spend an evening. Henry stood up and walked over toward the crater rim and called me over. "Anyela, come quickly." I dropped my fork immediately and walked over. What I witnessed will forever be etched in my mind. The steam appeared to have dissipated and a caldera of red-hot lava was bubbling below us. Bursts of fire exploded as the lava churned like a simmering pot of marinara sauce. Now I understood why Henry was so disappointed with our initial view! Henry, Damien, Peter and I sat up the entire night with our feet on the edge of the crater rim, watching the lava writhe with volatility. It was like watching the most epic campfire you've ever seen in your life under a canopy of stars. There was absolutely no way I was going to sleep and miss a single second of the experience. The heat from the lava could be felt almost 800 metres up on our feet. The constant churning rumble, periodically interrupted by a lava explosion with fire, was hypnotic. I sat in awe and appreciation for the ability and opportunity to be there, in that moment. I had a lot of people to thank for helping me get there safely.

Ironically, it was Henry who thanked me first. As we huddled together under a blanket he talked about how tourism has been negatively impacted by the circumstances in the Congo. He thanked me for taking the risk and having faith that there would be good people to help me and keep me safe. His appreciation was very humbling. I explained to him that I didn't want to put myself at risk, but I also didn't want to put anyone else at risk either. I was conflicted about the entire trip because of it. Henry put his hand on mine, looked me straight in the eyes and said that life can end at any time, without notice. So why not try? He then talked about how he lives in a country that does not allow him to travel freely and how it makes him happy to see someone using the freedoms they have to see the world. He thanked me one more time for visiting his country and said I'd be welcome back anytime. To keep things light, I joked and said I wasn't so sure the friendly visa folks would agree, but thank you.

The night felt like it passed so quickly. The sun came up and the steam settled inside the cauldron, hiding the lava from our view. Like watching the last tip of the sun fall into the ocean, I watched the last hint of red lava get swept over with steam. We had a quick breakfast, packed up the dishes and slung our backpacks over our shoulders. Henry gave me a nudge and poked fun at how I carried my bag up for no reason since I didn't use any of its contents. I joked that it was my plan all along so I could eat extra bananas. He laughed and offered some innocent advice: "Your bum is very small and you must move less to make it big. A big bum is good! You must eat a lot of bananas too." I laughed out loud at his suggestion. Everyone has an opinion! Gym humour, it's everywhere! I handed him my earbuds and MP3 player to listen to Sir Mix-A-Lot's "Baby Got Back." "Is this what you are talking about?" I asked while laughing. "Baby got back. Yes. This is very good music! I think he is a very smart man," Henry commented while he tried to listen and sing at the same time.

The four of us casually walked down the same switchbacks we came up the day before. It was another beautiful blue-sky day and the sun quickly became hot on my shoulders, but in a very pleasant way. Only a couple of times did Henry hear something that caused him to stop, pause and hold his hand out to me as a signal to be quiet. Damien and Peter would slowly walk ahead of us and then give us the nod that everything was fine. In just over an hour we were back down to the disconcerting bullet-holed welcome sign.

Julian and a couple of other gentlemen in dusty brown dress shirts, introduced as "colleagues," along with two military gentlemen, were waiting for us. Julian had a huge smile across his face. He seemed genuinely happy and relieved to see me healthy and well. "You look so fresh!" he said with glee as he gave me a big hug. "Did you see the crater? Oh my gawd, you are so fast!" His reaction in seeing me was overwhelming and gave me the impression we were very lucky to make it up and down with no issues. "Do you want a banana?" he asked. "You look skinny." I looked over at Henry to see if he had put Julian up to this. He grinned from ear to ear and couldn't contain himself. "Anyela, I am sorry, but it is so funny! Baby needs back!" I ran after Henry and attempted to tackle him to the ground. His slight physique was deceptively strong and he ended up tackling me. "Too skinny, Anyela." He grinned again, held out his hand to pull me up and gave me a bro hug.

We didn't hang around the area very long. Within ten minutes of arriving, all nine of us packed into two vehicles and convoyed back to Goma. We made a quick pit stop to drop off Damien, Peter, Henry and Julian's colleagues. I was asked not to get out of the vehicle to say my goodbyes, as this would attract too much attention, so I shook each of their hands and passed along a thank you note and an envelope of tips. I hoped they knew how appreciative I was. The parting was very quick and in some ways best. Goodbyes are tough for me.

There was no interest in spending extra time in Goma, for anyone. So we proceeded directly to the border crossing. Julian jumped out of the vehicle with my passport and made a beeline to the same building where he'd tackled the entry negotiations about 48 hours earlier. The military escorts said it was okay for me to get out and stretch my legs. "It will not be too long," they assured me. Julian waved me up to the building to join him. My passport was sitting open on the counter as I watched the departure stamp slam down and leave its ink stain. We did it.

Julian pulled my backpack out of the truck and proudly put it on my shoulders. It felt like he was more delighted with how well the trip went than even me. I shook his hand and passed along a thank you note and tip for him as well. He dove in and gave me a hug that was made a little more awkward with my backpack on. He directed me to walk to the guard on the right, hand him my stamped passport and then he'd permit me to cross over into Rwanda. I thanked Julian again for all of his assistance and expressed my gratitude for his genuine concern for my safety. He winked and told me I'd be welcome back anytime.

I made my way to the right and did exactly what Julian told me to do. The gentleman that flipped through my passport looked like he was about to let me through when another military-garbed man spoke to him in French and then directed me away from the gate into a concrete building behind us. He was speaking very fast and very loudly at me. I was desperately trying to understand what he was saying, while dealing with the knowledge that my passport was with the gentleman at the gate, and trying to calm him down all at the same time. I didn't think I had done anything wrong. I saw for myself the stamp in my passport. I had not purchased anything, so I had nothing to hide in that regard. My mind was racing with rational scenarios, but it was challenging when the man's voice became louder and more aggressive with each sentence.

When he discovered I couldn't communicate back, he yanked my backpack off me and threw it on the only table in the room. Another gentleman came in and the two of them pulled every item out of it to inspect what I had. My mind immediately went to a dark place. I started worrying about ridiculous situations like drugs being planted in my backpack and going to Congo prison, or having to pay these guys all of my money (or something worse) to cross the border. Or maybe they wouldn't let me leave? I just stepped back and let them tear everything apart while I observed the room. I had nothing to hide and I was thinking as fast as I could as to how I could get out of the building unharmed. *I can leave everything if I have to. My passport is outside of these four walls – that's all I really need to get out of here. Worst-case scenario, I have to run like mad and leave with just the shirt on my back. If it comes to that, I'll do it. Best-case scenario...* My thoughts were interrupted by an aggressive voice.

"Something, something, *le tabac!*" I heard from one of the men wearing dark sunglasses. "*Désolé, je ne parle pas francais,*" I said as clearly as I could to explain my French language inadequacy. He said it again, only louder and right in my face: "something, something, *le tabac!*" "I, I don't have any tobacco, er, *le tabac,*" I responded with the assumption he was asking for cigarettes. "I don't smoke. *Non, le tabac,*" I followed up with, hoping it would translate with some miracle. "Something, something, *le tabac!*" he said while he gritted his teeth. I shook my head in confusion and said with emotional restraint, "I don't have any. *Non!*" His partner, also wearing dark glasses, held up a Ziploc bag in front of me and hit me on the side of the face with it.

I looked at the bag in shock. And then, without any hesitation, I agreed they could have it. "*Oui,* you can have *le tabac.*" I nodded my head and gestured to them that it was all theirs as I spoke. They smiled at each other and stepped away from the table so I could grab my belongings and frantically shove them into my bag. I put the majority of the items inside and then tucked the rest under my armpit as I walked out of the building as fast as I could. There was no time to organize! I had to get out, *fast.*

Miraculously, the gentleman at the border gate held out my passport and let me through without any further questioning. Thank you, thank you, *thank you!* It was the smoothest transaction I had the entire trip and it couldn't have come at a better time. The second my feet hit the other side of the little metal gate, I knew I was going to be okay. I just needed to keep walking as fast as possible to increase the distance between us before they found anything out. I looked back over my shoulder to see if the guys were following me. *That's it, guys. Stay right there. Brag to your buddies.* One of them was gloating to the other men standing by, waving the Ziploc in the air and doing a little celebration dance. He pulled one of the yellow packages out of the baggie and placed it between his lips.

I wanted so badly to see the reaction on his face, but I couldn't take any more chances. It wouldn't be long before he realized he had a tampon in his mouth.

KENYA

Approximately 5:00 p.m.

UPON OUR ARRIVAL AT SAMUEL'S VILLAGE, he insisted on paying for my hostel room in town. Our mountain experience was negotiated in advance to include four nights and five days, but due to the harsh weather we completed the journey in one less day. I tried to convince him that it wasn't necessary to compensate me and that I was delighted to sleep in a warm place on night four, but he wouldn't have it. He passed his wet Kenyan shilling bills to the woman behind the desk and lifted my bag off my shoulders. "Let me take this for you," he kindly offered. Typically, I don't let anyone carry my bag for me. Remember Kilimanjaro? It's that independence thing I have. But in that moment, even with the knowledge of how bad Samuel's ankle was, I couldn't turn down his tenderhearted gesture and risk disrespecting him. "Thank you, Samuel."

We walked the six flights of stairs up to my hostel room floor and Samuel placed my bag on the ground at the end of the hall. Like the true gentleman he was, he didn't leave the option open to approach my room. "Cheese sandwich," he said good-heartedly and then winked. I smiled with delight and gave him a huge hug. "You were paying attention?" I said with delight and a little surprise. "Yes, I remember," he quickly responded back. "I will never forget you." We both knew we'd likely never see each other again, but we'd be forever connected. "I won't ever forget you either, Samuel. Thank you. Thank you for everything." "It is with pleasure. Be free, Anyela," he said as he shook my hand goodbye.

Afterword

TRAVELLING THROUGH AFRICA introduced me to myself. When everything was stripped away – distractions, job titles, education, vanity, dependencies, language, history, other's opinions, customs, expectations, biases, preconceptions and even my insecurities – I was left with just my gut instinct to guide me. Sometimes I was disappointed by it, other times I was pleasantly impressed.

I don't like every version of myself in these stories, and looking back I question many of the choices I made and how I handled some of the circumstances I was in. Would I go back and change them? Never. There were a few times while writing this book when I considered it, at least on paper, in order to make myself look less "stupid" or more "brave," but I didn't. Making mistakes is an important part of life and one of the best ways to learn and grow. I coach my personal training clients and remind them often that we are products of our choices – including the bad ones. Editing my errors and poor decisions would have been dishonest to you, the reader, and a dishonour to myself. Acknowledging the good, the bad and the ugly in our experiences and reactions to them is important, because they ultimately shape us as unique individuals. It's what makes us all interesting.

Thank you for taking the time to read my stories. They were certainly fun to live and then relive while writing.

If you decide you want to climb your own mountains but don't know where to start, my book *Polepole: A Training Guide for Kilimanjaro and Other Long-Distance Mountain Treks*, co-authored with Erinne Sevigny Adachi, will provide the fitness guidance you need to do it. After that, all that's required are a plane ticket, a reliable coat and an open mind to have the adventure of a lifetime.

I'll leave you with my top ten lessons from these adventures. They have shaped me into the person I am today and I'm truly grateful to have been open to receiving them. In no particular order:

1. Life is about evolving, not accumulating: get out and learn.
2. People, in general, are good: they want to share; they want to help.
3. Weather and altitude must be taken seriously: what you wear matters, and symptom recognition is critical.
4. Food and clean water are a privilege: don't take them for granted, or waste them.
5. Your gut instinct is likely right (for you) 99 per cent of the time.
6. Vulnerability is the key to self-discovery: get uncomfortable.
7. A fit body can offer possibilities you never imagined: move your muscles.
8. Attitude and perspective can make or break you: choose wisely.
9. Listen: it is the single best way to learn.
10. It's your life to live: do it the way you want. Be free.

Acknowledgements

THANK YOU to the Rocky Mountain Books publishing team for investing in this book and making the experience comfortable, encouraging and seamless right from the start. It's not easy to be vulnerable and press "Send" with a manuscript containing a collection of some of your most personal memories. I'm grateful to have had the opportunity to work together on a second project and appreciate the support I've been given along the way.

A heartfelt thanks to Don Gorman for seeing the possibilities, right away, in *Be Free*. I'd also like to thank Don for his reassuring communication updates to all the RMB authors during each stage of the publishing process at a stressful and uncertain time during the COVID-19 pandemic. To Kirsten Craven, a gracious thank you for your quick turnaround and sensitive approach to the editing process. We may not have always agreed on how many exclamation points were necessary, but you were an absolute joy to work with!

To Erinne Sevigny Adachi, thank you for being the first person to welcome me into this publishing world. You may not have been involved directly with this project, but you were still a contributor to it with all the guidance you've given me over the years. I'm very thankful for your advice, your continued support and your friendship.

I have the pleasure of waking up every day to train with some of the most inspiring, hard-working people I've ever known: my clients and friends. Fitness is such a big part of my life, and I am honoured to share it with you and witness how it continues to transform your lives. Thank you for your trust, your commitment and your time. It's a privilege to be in your company each week. I'm also grateful for your cautious yet understanding support for my adventures, and your genuine happiness for me.

A sincere thank you to all the gentlemen and ladies I've met while abroad that have treated me like a friend or family member, instantly. I tear up just thinking about the generosity and kindness I've been given from so many strangers over the years, regardless of our lack of ability to communicate verbally.

To all the climbing guides, cooks, rangers and drivers I've met along the way, thank you. I know for most of you this was not your profession but rather a way to make extra money for your families, but you gave me the adventures of a lifetime. Your companionship, genuine concern for my safety and openness to drag a strange, solo, foreigner lady up the side of a volcano is something I will be forever grateful for. If it were not for you fellas, and your knowledge of the area, I wouldn't have made it. No amount of fitness can combat the African wilderness.

Thank you to Jan and Marge, my favourite brother and incredible friends for believing in me. I don't often share a lot about myself, so I realize many of these stories will come as a shock when you read them. Just know that your love and support gave me strength during some of the hardest times.

Thank you to my favourite mom and favourite dad for encouraging me to see the world and experience all it has to offer. One of the greatest gifts you've given me is curiosity. You've also taught me to work hard, to keep learning, to listen and to trust that it will all work out the way it should. I know some of my timing and destination choices were questionable, but instead of talking me out of it, you led by example and asked questions, listened and trusted my ability to make the right decisions. I love you and am so grateful for everything you've done for me and continue to do.

To my husband Mike, there is only one feeling in this world better than being loved. It is knowing that you're understood. Thank you for always supporting my adventurous spirit and having unwavering confidence in my ability, even when I've not been convinced of it myself. You are my biggest cheerleader and my best friend. I love you so much, and I am honoured you wanted to share your life with me.

Finally, thank you to Larry, our cat. You've sat on my lap for endless hours, causing me to happily contort my body to accommodate you and still manage to type the manuscript off to the side. You have been with me for every single thought put on these pages. You are a devoted, warm, sleepy companion that melts my heart.